TABE® REVIEW

Test of Adult Basic Education
Study Guide and
Practice Test Questions

Copyright © 2014 by Complete Test Preparation Inc. ALL RIGHTS RESERVED. No part of this book may be reproduced or transferred in any form or by any means, graphic, electronic, or mechanical, including photocopying, recording, web distribution, taping, or by any information storage retrieval system, without the written permission of the author.

Notice: Complete Test Preparation Inc. makes every reasonable effort to obtain from reliable sources accurate, complete, and timely information about the tests covered in this book. Nevertheless, changes can be made in the tests or the administration of the tests at any time and Complete Test Preparation Inc. makes no representation or warranty, either expressed or implied as to the accuracy, timeliness, or completeness of the information contained in this book. Complete Test Preparation Inc. makes no representations or warranties of any kind, express or implied, about the completeness, accuracy, reliability, suitability or availability with respect to the information contained in this document for any purpose. Any reliance you place on such information is therefore strictly at your own risk.

The author(s) shall not be liable for any loss incurred as a consequence of the use and application, directly or indirectly, of any information presented in this work. Sold with the understanding, the author(s) is not engaged in rendering professional services or advice. If advice or expert assistance is required, the services of a competent professional should be sought.

The company, product and service names used in this publication are for identification purposes only. All trademarks and registered trademarks are the property of their respective owners. Complete Test Preparation Inc. is not affiliated with any educational institution.

We strongly recommend that students check with exam providers for up-to-date information regarding test content.

TABE® and the Test of Adult Basic Education is a registered trademark of the MCGRAW-HILL, INC. who are not involved in the production of, and do not endorse this product.

ISBN-13: 9781772450712

Version 7.8 Updated February 2020

Published by
Complete Test Preparation Inc.
Victoria BC Canada
Visit us on the web at https://www.test-preparation.ca
Printed in the USA

About Complete Test Preparation Inc.

The Complete Test Preparation Team has been publishing high quality study materials since 2005. Over two million students visit our websites every year, and thousands of students, teachers and parents all over the world (over 100 countries) have purchased our teaching materials, curriculum, study guides and practice tests.

Complete Test Preparation Inc. is committed to providing students with the best study materials and practice tests available on the market. Members of our team combine years of teaching experience, with experienced writers and editors, all with advanced degrees.

Feedback

We welcome your feedback. Email us at feedback@test-preparation.ca with your comments and suggestions. We carefully review all suggestions and often incorporate reader suggestions into upcoming versions. As a Print on Demand Publisher, we update our products frequently.

Contents

6 Getting Started
How this study guide is organized 7
The TABE® Study Plan 8
Making a Study Schedule 8

14 Reading
Self-Assessment 18
Answer Key 26
Help with Reading Comprehension 29
Main Idea, Topic and Supporting Details 32

36 Computational Mathematics
Self-Assessment 40
Answer Key 47
Basic Math Video Tutorials 49
Fraction Tips, Tricks and Shortcuts 49
Converting Fractions to Decimals 52
Decimal Tips, Tricks and Shortcuts 55
Converting Decimals to Fractions 55
Percent Tips, Tricks and Shortcuts 56
Exponents: Tips, Shortcuts & Tricks 58
Order Of Operation 63

65 Applied Mathematics
Self Assessment 69
Answer Key 75
How to Solve Word Problems 79
Types of Word Problems 82
Ratio 91
Pythagorean Geometry 97

100 Language
Self-Assessment 104
Answer Key 117
Grammar and Punctuation Tutorials 121
Capitalization 121
Colons and Semicolons 123
Commas 124
English Grammar Multiple Choice 127
Common English Usage Mistakes 144
Subject Verb Agreement 151

161 **Practice Test Questions Set 1**
Answer Key 209

225 **Practice Test Questions Set 2**
Answer Key 271

287 **Conclusion**

289 **Online Resources**

https://www.facebook.com/CompleteTestPreparation/

https://www.youtube.com/user/MrTestPreparation

Getting Started

CONGRATULATIONS! By deciding to take the Test of Adult Basic Education (TABE®), you have taken the first step toward a great future! Of course, there is no point in taking this important examination unless you intend to do your best to earn the highest grade you possibly can. That means getting yourself organized and discovering the best approaches, methods and strategies to master the material. Yes, that will require real effort and dedication on your part, but if you are willing to focus your energy and devote the study time necessary, before you know it you will be on you way to a brighter future.

We know that taking on a new endeavour can be scary, and it is easy to feel unsure of where to begin. That's where we come in. This study guide is designed to help you improve your test-taking skills, show you a few tricks of the trade and increase both your competency and confidence.

The Test of Adult Basic Education®

The TABE® exam is a computer based exam, composed of four sections, reading, computational mathematics, applied mathematics, and language.

Section	Time	Questions
Reading	25	25
Computational Math	15	25
Applied Math	25	25
Language	25	25

For complete details on the skills evaluated in each section, see the corresponding chapter below.

While we seek to make our guide as comprehensive as possible, note that like all entrance exams, the TABE® Exam might be adjusted at some future point. New material might be added, or content that is no longer relevant or applicable might be removed. It is always a good idea to give the materials you receive when you register to take the TABE® a careful review.

How this study guide is organized

This study guide is divided into three sections. The first section, Self-Assessments, which will help you recognize your areas of strength and weaknesses. This will be a boon when it comes to managing your study time most efficiently; there is not much point of focusing on material you have already got firmly under control. Instead, taking the self-assessments will show you where that time could be much better spent. In this area you will begin with a few questions to quickly evaluate your understanding of material that is likely to appear on the TABE®. If you do poorly in certain areas, simply work carefully through those sections in the tutorials and then try the self-assessment again.

The second section, Tutorials, offers information in each of the content areas, as well as strategies to help you master that material. The tutorials are not intended to be a complete course, but cover general principles. If you find that you do not understand the tutorials, it is recommended that you seek out additional instruction. Most Universities recommend student take introductory courses in Math, English and Science before taking the TABE®.

Third, we offer two sets of practice test questions, similar to those on the TABE® Exam. Again, we cover all modules, so make sure to check with your school!

The TABE® Study Plan

Now that you have made the decision to take the TABE®, it is time to get started. Before you do another thing, you will need to figure out a plan of attack. The very best study tip is to start early! The longer the time period you devote to regular study practice, the more likely you will retain the material and access it quickly. If you thought that 1x20 is the same as 2x10, guess what? It really is not, when it comes to study time. Reviewing material for just an hour per day over the course of 20 days is far better than studying for two hours a day for only 10 days. The more often you revisit a particular piece of information, the better you will know it. Not only will your grasp and understanding be better, but your ability to reach into your brain and quickly and efficiently pull out the tidbit you need, will be greatly enhanced as well.

The great Chinese scholar and philosopher Confucius believed that true knowledge could be defined as knowing what you know and what you do not know. The first step in preparing for the TABE® Exam is to assess your strengths and weaknesses. You may already have an idea of what you know and what you do not know, but evaluating yourself using our Self- Assessment modules for each of the three areas, math, reading comprehension and essay writing, will clarify the details.

Making a Study Schedule

To make your study time the most productive, you will need to develop a study plan. The purpose of the plan is to organize all the bits of pieces of information in such a way that you will not feel overwhelmed. Rome was not built in a day, and learning everything you will need to know to pass the TABE® Exam is going to take time, too. Arranging the material you need to learn into manageable chunks is the best way to go. Each study session should make you feel as though you have accomplished your goal, or at least are a little closer, and your goal is simply to learn what you planned to learn during that particular session. Try to organize the content in such a way that each study session builds upon previous ones. That way, you will retain the information, be better able to access it, and review the previous bits and pieces at the same time.

Self-assessment

The Best Study Tip! The very best study tip is to start early! The longer you study regularly, the more you will retain and 'learn' the material. Studying for 1 hour per day for 20 days is far better than studying for 2 hours for 10 days.

What don't you know?

The first step is to assess your strengths and weaknesses. You may already have an idea of where your weaknesses are, or you can take our Self-assessment modules for each of the areas, math, reading comprehension and essay writing.

Exam Component	Rate from 1 to 5
Reading	
Main idea and supporting details	
Drawing inferences	
Mathematics	
Algebra	
Estimation	
Percent, Decimal, Fractions	
Word Problems	
Basic Geometry	
Word Problems	

Making a Study Schedule

The key to a successful study plan is to divide the material you need to learn into manageable size and learn it, while at the same time reviewing the material that you already know.

Using the table above, any scores of three or below, mean you need to spend time learning, going over, and practicing this subject area. A score of four means you need to review the material, but you don't have to spend time re-learning. A score of five and you are OK with just an occasional review before the exam.

A score of zero or one means you really do need to work on this and you should allocate the most time and give it the highest priority. Some students prefer a 5-day plan and others a 10-day plan. It also depends on how much time you have until the exam.

Here is an example of a 5-day plan based on an example from the table above:

Reading: 1   Study 1 hour everyday – review on last day
Fractions: 3   Study 1 hour for 2 days then ½ hour and then review
Algebra: 4   Review every second day
Word Problems (Applied Math) : 2 Study 1 hour on the first day – then ½ hour everyday
Basic Geometry: 5 Review for ½ hour every other day

Using this example, Basic Geometry is good and only needs occasional review. Algebra is good and needs 'some' review. Fractions need a bit of work, grammar and usage needs a lot of work and Reading is very weak and need the most time. Based on this, here is a sample study plan:

Day	Subject	Time
Monday		
Study	Reading	1 hour
Study	Word Problems	1 hour
	½ hour break	
Study	Fractions	1 hour
Review	Algebra	½ hour
Tuesday		
Study	Reading	1 hour
Study	Word Problems	½ hour
	½ hour break	
Study	Fractions	½ hour
Review	Algebra	½ hour
Review	Basic Geometry	½ hour
Wednesday		
Study	Reading	1 hour
Study	Word Problems	½ hour
	½ hour break	
Study	Fractions	½ hour
Review	Basic Geometry	½ hour
Thursday		
Study	Reading	½ hour
Study	Word Problems	½ hour
Review	Fractions	½ hour
	½ hour break	
Review	Basic Geometry	½ hour
Review	Algebra	½ hour
Friday		
Review	Reading	½ hour
Review	Word Problems	½ hour
Review	Fractions	½ hour
	½ hour break	
Review	Algebra	½ hour
Review	Word Problems	½ hour

Using this example, adapt the study plan to your own schedule. This schedule assumes 2 ½ - 3 hours available to study everyday for a 5 day period.

First, write out what you need to study and how much. Next figure out how many days you have before the test. Note, do NOT study on the last day before the test. On the last day before the test, you won't learn anything and will probably only confuse yourself.

Make a table with the days before the test and the number of hours you have available to study each day. We suggest working with 1 hour and ½ hour time slots.

Start filling in the blanks, with the subjects you need to study the most getting the most time and the most regular time slots (i.e. everyday) and the subjects that you know getting the least time (e.g. ½ hour every other day, or every 3rd day).

Tips for making a schedule

Once you make a schedule, stick with it! Make your study sessions reasonable. If you make a study schedule and don't stick with it, you set yourself up for failure. Instead, schedule study sessions that are a bit shorter and set yourself up for success! Make sure your study sessions are do-able. Studying is hard work but after you pass, you can party and take a break!

Schedule breaks. Breaks are just as important as study time. Work out a rotation of studying and breaks that works for you.

Build up study time. If you find it hard to sit still and study for 1 hour straight through, build up to it. Start with 20 minutes, and then take a break. Once you get used to 20-minute study sessions, increase the time to 30 minutes. Gradually work you way up to 1 hour.

40 minutes to 1 hour is optimal. Studying for longer than this is tiring and not productive. Studying for shorter isn't long enough to be productive.

Studying Math. Studying Math is different from studying other subjects because you use a different part of your brain. The best way to study math is to practice everyday. This will train your mind to think in a mathematical way. If you miss a day or days, the mathematical mind-set is gone and you have to start all over again to build it up.

Study and practice math everyday for at least 5 days before the exam.

Reading

THIS SECTION CONTAINS A SELF-ASSESSMENT AND READING TUTORIAL. The Tutorials are designed to familiarize general principles and the self-assessment contains general questions similar to the reading questions likely to be on the TABE® exam, but are not intended to be identical to the exam questions. The tutorials are not designed to be a complete reading course, and it is assumed that students have some familiarity with reading comprehension questions. If you do not understand parts of the tutorial, or find the tutorial difficult, it is recommended that you seek out additional instruction.

Note that these questions are for skill practice only.

Tour of the TABE® Reading Content

The TABE® reading section has 50 reading questions. Below is a detailed list of the types of reading questions that generally appear on the TABE®.

- Evaluating meaning
- Drawing inferences
- Identifying main ideas and supporting detail

The questions below are not the same as you will find on the TABE® - that would be too easy! And nobody knows what the questions will be and they change all the time. Mostly the changes consist of substituting new questions for old, but the changes can be new question formats or styles, changes to the number of questions in each section, changes to the time limits for each section and combining sections. Below are general reading questions that cover the same areas as the TABE®. So, while the format and exact wording of the questions may differ slightly, and change from year to year, if you can answer the questions below, you will have no problem with the reading section of the TABE®.

Reading Self-Assessment

The purpose of the self-assessment is:

- Identify your strengths and weaknesses.
- Develop your personalized study plan (above)
- Get accustomed to the TABE® format
- Extra practice – the self-assessments are almost a full 3rd practice test!
- Provide a baseline score for preparing your study schedule.

Since this is a Self-assessment, and depending on how confident you are with reading comprehension, timing is optional. The TABE® has 25 reading questions to be completed in 25 minutes. The self-assessment has 15 questions, so allow about 15 minutes to complete this assessment.

Once complete, use the table below to assess your understanding of the content, and prepare your study schedule described in chapter 1.

80% - 100%	Excellent – you have mastered the content
60 – 79%	Good. You have a working knowledge. Even though you can just pass this section, you may want to review the Tutorials and do some extra practice to see if you can improve your mark.
40% - 59%	Below Average. You do not understand reading questions. Review the tutorials, and retake this quiz again in a few days, before proceeding to the rest of the practice test questions.
Less than 40%	Poor. You have a very limited understanding of reading questions. Please review the tutorials, and retake this quiz again in a few days, before proceeding to the practice test questions.

Self-Assessment Answer Sheet

	A	B	C	D
1	○	○	○	○
2	○	○	○	○
3	○	○	○	○
4	○	○	○	○
5	○	○	○	○
6	○	○	○	○
7	○	○	○	○
8	○	○	○	○
9	○	○	○	○
10	○	○	○	○
11	○	○	○	○
12	○	○	○	○
13	○	○	○	○
14	○	○	○	○
15	○	○	○	○

Directions: The following questions are based on several reading passages. A series of questions follow each passage. Read each passage carefully, and then answer the questions based on it. You may reread the passage as often as you wish. When you have finished answering the questions based on one passage, go right onto the next passage. Choose the best answer based on the information given and implied.

Questions 1 – 4 refer to the following passage.

Passage 1 - Who Was Anne Frank?

You may have heard mention of the word Holocaust in your History or English classes. The Holocaust took place from 1939-1945. It was an attempt by the Nazi party to purify the human race, by eliminating Jews, Gypsies, Catholics, homosexuals and others they deemed inferior to their "perfect" Aryan race. The Nazis used Concentration Camps, which were sometimes used as Death Camps, to exterminate the people they held in the camps. The saddest fact about the Holocaust was the over one million children under the age of sixteen died in a Nazi concentration camp. Just a few weeks before World War II was over, Anne Frank was one of those children to die.

Before the Nazi party began its persecution of the Jews, Anne Frank had a happy live. She was born in June of 1929. In June of 1942, for her 13th birthday, she was given a simple present which would go onto impact the lives of millions of people around the world. That gift was a small red diary that she called Kitty. This diary was to become Anne's most treasured possession when she and her family hid from the Nazi's in a secret annex above her father's office building in Amsterdam.

For 25 months, Anne, her sister Margot, her parents, another family, and an elderly Jewish dentist hid from the Nazis in this tiny annex. They were never permitted to go outside, and their food and supplies were brought to them by Miep Gies and her husband, who did not believe in the Nazi persecution of the Jews. It was a very difficult life for young Anne and she used Kitty as an outlet to describe her life in hiding.

After 2 years, Anne and her family were betrayed and arrested by the Nazis. To this day, nobody is exactly sure who betrayed the Frank family and the other annex residents. Anne, her mother, and her sister were separated from Otto Frank, Anne's father. Then, Anne and Margot were separated from their mother. In March of 1945, Margot Frank died of starvation in a Concentration Camp. A few days later, at the age of 15, Anne Frank died of typhus. Of all the people who hid in the Annex, only Otto Frank survived the Holocaust.

Otto Frank returned to the Annex after World War II. It was there that he found Kitty, filled with Anne's thoughts and feelings about being a persecuted Jewish girl. Otto Frank had Anne's diary published in 1947 and it has remained continuously in print ever since. Today, the diary has been published in over 55 languages and more than 24 million copies have been sold around the world. The Diary of Anne Frank tells the story of a brave young woman who tried to see the good in all people.

1. From the context clues in the passage, what does annex mean?

    a. Attic

    b. Bedroom

    c. Basement

    d. Kitchen

2. Why do you think Anne's diary has been published in 55 languages?

    a. So everyone could understand it.

    b. So people around the world could learn more about the horrors of the Holocaust.

    c. Because Anne was Jewish but hid in Amsterdam and died in Germany.

    d. Because Otto Frank spoke many languages.

3. From the description of Anne and Margot's deaths in the passage, what can we assume typhus is?

   a. The same as starving to death.

   b. An infection the Germans gave to Anne.

   c. A disease Anne caught in the concentration camp.

   d. Poison gas used by the Germans to kill Anne.

4. In the third paragraph, what does outlet mean?

   a. A place to plug things into the wall

   b. A store where Miep bought cheap supplies for the Frank family

   c. A hiding space similar to an Annex

   d. A place where Anne could express her private thoughts.

Questions 5 – 8 refer to the following passage.

Passage 2 - Was Dr. Seuss A Real Doctor?

A favorite author for over 100 years, Theodor Seuss Geisel was born on March 2, 1902. Today, we celebrate the birthday of the famous "Dr. Seuss" by hosting Read Across America events throughout the March. School children around the country celebrate the "Doctor's" birthday by making hats, giving presentations and holding read aloud circles featuring some of Dr. Seuss' most famous books.

But who was Dr. Seuss? Did he go to medical school? Where was his office? You may be surprised to know that Theodor Seuss Geisel was not a medical doctor at all. He took on the nickname Dr. Seuss when he became a noted children's book author. He earned the nickname because people said his books were "as good as medicine." All these years later, his nickname has lasted and he is known as Dr. Seuss all across the world.

Think back to when you were a young child. Did you ever

want to try "green eggs and ham?" Did you try to "Hop on Pop?" Do you remember learning about the environment from a creature called The Lorax? Of course, you must recall one of Seuss' most famous characters; that green Grinch who stole Christmas. These stories were all written by Dr. Seuss and featured his signature rhyming words and letters. They also featured made up words to enhance his rhyme scheme and even though many of his characters were made up, they sure seem real to us today.

And what of his "signature" book, The Cat in the Hat? You must remember that cat and Thing One and Thing Two from your childhood. Did you know that in the early 1950's there was a growing concern in America that children were not becoming avid readers? This was, book publishers thought, because children found books dull and uninteresting. An intelligent publisher sent Dr. Seuss a book of words that he thought all children should learn as young readers. Dr. Seuss wrote his famous story The Cat in the Hat, using those words. We can see, over the decades, just how much influence his writing has had on very young children. That is why we celebrate this doctor's birthday each March.

5. What does the word "avid" mean in the last paragraph?

    a. Good

    b. Interested

    c. Slow

    d. Fast

6. What can we infer from the statement " His books were like medicine?"

    a. His books made people feel better

    b. His books were in doctor's office waiting rooms

    c. His books took away fevers

    d. His books left a funny taste in readers' mouths.

7. Why is the publisher in the last paragraph called "intelligent?"

   a. The publisher knew how to read.

   b. The publisher knew that kids did not like to read.

   c. The publisher knew Dr. Seuss would be able to create a book that sold well.

   d. The publisher knew that Dr. Seuss would be able to write a book that would get young children interested in reading.

8. The theme of this passage is

   a. Dr. Seuss was not a doctor.

   b. Dr. Seuss influenced the lives of generations of young children.

   c. Dr. Seuss wrote rhyming books.

   d. Dr. Suess' birthday is a good day to read a book.

Questions 9 - 12 refer to the following passage.

Keeping Tropical Fish

Keeping tropical fish at home or in your office used to be very popular. Today, interest has declined, but it remains as rewarding and relaxing a hobby as ever. Ask any tropical fish hobbyist, and you will hear how soothing and relaxing watching colorful fish live their lives in the aquarium. If you are considering keeping tropical fish as pets, here is a list of the basic equipment you will need.

A filter is essential for keeping your aquarium clean and your fish alive and healthy. There are different types and sizes of filters and the right size for you depends on the size of the aquarium and the level of stocking. Generally, you need a filter with a 3 to 5 times turn over rate per hour. This means that the water in the tank should go through the filter about 3 to 5 times per hour.

Most tropical fish do well in water temperatures ranging between 24° C and 26° C, though each has its own ideal water temperature. A heater with a thermostat is necessary to regulate the water temperature. Some heaters are submersible and others are not, so check carefully before you buy.

Lights are also necessary, and come in a large variety of types, strengths and sizes. A light source is necessary for plants in the tank to photosynthesize and give the tank a more attractive appearance. Even if you plan to use plastic plants, the fish still require light, although here you can use a lower strength light source.

A hood is necessary to keep dust, dirt and unwanted materials out of the tank. Sometimes the hood can also help prevent evaporation. Another requirement is aquarium gravel. This will improve the aesthetics of the aquarium and is necessary if you plan to have real plants.

9. What is the general tone of this article?

    a. Formal

    b. Informal

    c. Technical

    d. Opinion

10. Which of the following cannot be inferred?

    a. Gravel is good for aquarium plants.

    b. Fewer people have aquariums in their office than at home.

    c. The larger the tank, the larger the filter required.

    d. None of the above.

11. What evidence does the author provide to support their claim that aquarium lights are necessary?

    a. Plants require light.

    b. Fish and plants require light.

    c. The author does not provide evidence for this statement.

    d. Aquarium lights make the aquarium more attractive.

12. Which of the following is an opinion?

    a. Filter with a 3 to 5 times turn over rate per hour are required.

    b. Aquarium gravel improves the aesthetics of the aquarium.

    c. An aquarium hood keeps dust, dirt and unwanted materials out of the tank.

    d. Each type of tropical fish has its own ideal water temperature.

Questions 13 - 15 refer to the following passage.

The Civil War

The Civil War began on April 12, 1861. The first shots of the Civil War were fired in Fort Sumter, South Carolina. Note that even though more American lives were lost in the Civil War than in any other war, not one person died on that first day. The war began because eleven Southern states seceded from the Union and tried to start their own government, The Confederate States of America.

Why did the states secede? The issue of slavery was a primary cause of the Civil War. The eleven southern states relied heavily on their slaves to foster their farming and plantation lifestyles. The northern states, many of whom had already abolished slavery, did not feel that the southern states should have slaves. The north wanted to free all the slaves and President Lincoln's goal was to both end slavery and preserve the Union. He had Congress declare war on the Confederacy on April 14, 1862. For four long, blood soaked years, the North and South fought.

From 1861 to mid 1863, it seemed as if the South would win this war. However, on July 1, 1863, an epic three day battle was waged on a field in Gettysburg, Pennsylvania. Gettysburg is remembered for being the bloodiest battle in American history. At the end of the three days, the North turned the tide of the war in their favor. The North then went on to

dominate the South for the remainder of the war. A famous episode is General Sherman's "March to The Sea," where he famously led the Union Army through Georgia and the Carolinas, burning and destroying everything in their path.
In 1865, the Union army invaded and captured the Confederate capital of Richmond Virginia. Robert E. Lee, leader of the Confederacy surrendered to General Ulysses S. Grant, leader of the Union forces, on April 9, 1865. The Civil War was over and the Union was preserved.

13. What does secede mean?

    a. To break away from

    b. To accomplish

    c. To join

    d. To lose

14. Which of the following statements summarizes a FACT from the passage?

    a. Congress declared war and then the Battle of Fort Sumter began.

    b. Congress declared war after shots were fired at Fort Sumter.

    c. President Lincoln was pro slavery

    d. President Lincoln was at Fort Sumter with Congress

15. Which event finally led the Confederacy to surrender?

    a. The battle of Gettysburg

    b. The battle of Bull Run

    c. The invasion of the confederate capital of Richmond

    d. Sherman's March to the Sea

Answer Key

1. A
We know that an annex is like an attic because the text states the annex was above Otto Frank's building.

Choice B is incorrect because an office building doesn't have bedrooms. Choice C is incorrect because a basement would be below the office building. Choice D is incorrect because there would not be a kitchen in an office building.

2. B
The diary has been published in 55 languages so people all over the world can learn about Anne. That is why the passage says it has been continuously in print.

Choice A is incorrect because it is too vague. Choice C is incorrect because it was published after Anne died and she did not write in all three languages. Choice D is incorrect because the passage does not give us any information about what languages Otto Frank spoke.

3. C
Use the process of elimination to figure this out.

Choice A cannot be the correct answer because otherwise the passage would have simply said that Anne and Margot both died of starvation. Choices B and D cannot be correct because if the Germans had done something specifically to murder Anne, the passage would have stated that directly. By the process of elimination, choice C has to be the correct answer.

4. D
We can figure this out using context clues. The paragraph is talking about Anne's diary and so, outlet in this instance is a place where Anne can pour her feelings.

Choice A is incorrect answer. That is the literal meaning of the word outlet and the passage is using the figurative meaning. Choice B is incorrect because that is the secondary literal meaning of the word outlet, as in an outlet mall. Again, we are looking for figurative meaning. Choice C is incorrect because

there are no clues in the text to support that answer.
5. B
When someone is avid about something that means they are highly interested in the subject. The context clues are dull and boring, because they define the opposite of avid.

6. A
The author is using a simile to compare the books to medicine. Medicine is what you take when you want to feel better. They are suggesting that if a person wants to feel good, they should read Dr. Seuss' books.

Choice B is incorrect because there is no mention of a doctor's office. Choice C is incorrect because it is using the literal meaning of medicine and the author is using medicine in a figurative way. Choice D is incorrect because it makes no sense. We know not to eat books.

7. D
The publisher is described as intelligent because he knew to get in touch with a famous author to develop a book that children would be interested in reading.

Choice A is incorrect because we can assume that all book publishers must know how to read. Choice B is incorrect because it says in the article that more than one publisher was concerned about whether or not children liked to read. Choice C is incorrect because there is no mention in the article about how well The Cat in the Hat sold when it was first published.

8. B
The passage describes in detail how Dr. Seuss had a great effect on the lives of children through his writing. It names several of his books, tells how he helped children become avid readers and explains his style of writing.

Choice A is incorrect because that is just one single fact about the passage. Choice C is incorrect because that is just one single fact about the passage. Choice D is incorrect because that is just one single fact about the passage. Again, choice B is correct because it encompasses ALL the facts in the passage, not just one single fact.

9. B
The general tone is informal.

10. B
The statement, "Fewer people have aquariums in their office than at home," cannot be inferred from this article.

11. B
Light is necessary for the fish and plants.

12. B
The following statement is an opinion, " Aquarium gravel improves the aesthetics of the aquarium."

13. A
Secede means to break away from because the 11 states wanted to leave the United States and form their own country.

Choice B is incorrect because the states were not accomplishing anything. Choice C is incorrect because the states were trying to leave the USA not join it. Choice D is incorrect because the states seceded before they lost the war.

14. B
Look at the dates in the passage. The shots were fired on April 12 and Congress declared war on April 14.

Choice C is incorrect because the passage states that Lincoln was against slavery. Choice D is incorrect because it never mentions who was or was not at Fort Sumter.

15. C
The passage states that Lee surrendered to Grant after the capture of the capital of the Confederacy, which is Richmond.

Choice A is incorrect because the war continued for 2 years after Gettysburg. Choice B is incorrect because that battle is not mentioned in the passage. Choice D is incorrect because the capture of the capital occurred after the march to the sea.

Help with Reading Comprehension

At first sight, reading comprehension tests look challenging especially if you are given long essays to answer only two to three questions. While reading, you might notice your attention wandering, or you may feel sleepy. Do not be discouraged because there are various tactics and long-range strategies that make comprehending even long, boring essays easier.

Your friends before your foes. It is always best to start with passages with familiar subjects rather than those with unfamiliar ones. This approach applies the same logic as tackling easy questions before hard ones. Skip passages that do not interest you and leave them for later.

Don't use 'special' reading techniques. This is not the time for speed-reading or anything like that – just plain ordinary reading – not too slow and not too fast.

Read through the entire passage and the questions before you do anything. Many students try reading the questions first and then looking for answers in the passage thinking this approach is more efficient. What these students do not realize is that it is often hard to navigate in unfamiliar roads. If you do not familiarize yourself with the passage first, looking for answers become not only time-consuming but also dangerous because you might miss the context of the answer you are looking for. If you read the questions first you will only confuse yourself and lose valuable time.

Familiarize yourself with Reading Comprehension questions. If you are familiar with the common types of reading questions, you are able to take note of important parts of the passage, saving time. There are six major kinds of reading questions.

- **Main Idea**- Questions that ask for the central thought or significance of the passage.

- **Specific Details** - Questions that asks for explicitly

stated ideas.

- **Drawing Inferences** - Questions that ask for a logical extension of statements.

- **Tone or Attitude** - Questions that test your ability to sense the emotional state of the author.

- **Context Meaning** – Questions that ask for the meaning of a word depending on the context.

- **Technique** – Questions that ask for the method of organization or the writing style of the author.

Read. Read. Read. The best preparation for Reading Comprehension tests is always to read, read and read. If you are not used to reading lengthy passages, you will probably lose concentration. Increase your attention span by making a habit out of reading. Read everyday and increase the time slowly each day.

Reading comprehension tests become less daunting when you have trained yourself to read and understand fast. Always remember that it is easier to understand passages you are interested in. Do not read through passages hastily. Make mental notes of ideas you may be asked.

Reading Comprehension Strategy

When facing the reading comprehension section of a standardized test, you need a strategy to be successful. You want to keep several steps in mind:

- **First, make a note of the time and the number of sections.** Time your work accordingly. Typically, four to five minutes per section is sufficient. Second, read the directions for each selection thoroughly before beginning (and listen carefully to any additional verbal instructions, as they will often clarify obscure or confusing written guidelines). You must know exactly how to do what you're about to do!

- **Now you're ready to begin reading the selection.** Read the passage carefully, noting significant characters or events on scrap paper or underlining on the test sheet. Many students find making a basic list in the margins helpful. Quickly jot down or underline one-word summaries of characters, notable happenings, numbers, or key ideas. This will help retain information and focus wandering thoughts. Remember, however, that your goal is to find the information that answers the questions. Even if you find the passage interesting, stay on track.

- **Now read the question and all the choices.** Now you have read the passage, have a general idea of the main ideas, and have marked the important points. Read the question and all the choices. Never choose an answer without reading them all! Questions are often designed to confuse – stay focussed and clear. Usually the answer choices will focus on one or two facts or inferences from the passage. Keep these clear in your mind.

- **Search for the answer.** With a very general idea of what the different choices are, go back to the passage and scan for the relevant information. Watch for big words, unusual or unique words. These make your job easier as you can scan the text for the particular word.

- **Mark the Answer.** Now you have the key information the question is looking for. Go back to the question, quickly scan the choices and mark the correct one.

Typically, there will be several questions dealing with facts from the selection, a couple more inference questions dealing with logical consequences of those facts, and periodically an application-oriented question surfaces to force you to make connections with what you already know. Some students prefer to answer the questions as listed, and feel classifying the question and then ordering is wasting precious time. Other students prefer to answer the different types of questions in order of how easy or difficult they are. The choice is yours and do whatever works for you. If you want to try answering in order of difficulty, here is a recommended order, answer fact questions first; they're easily found within the passage. Tackle inference problems next, after re-reading the question(s) as many times as you need to. Application or 'best guess' questions usually take the longest, so, save them for last.

Use the practice tests to try out both ways of answering and see what works for you.

For more help with Reading Comprehension, see Multiple Choice Secrets, at www.multiple-choice.ca

Main Idea, Topic and Supporting Details

Identifying the main idea, topic and supporting details in a passage can feel like an overwhelming task. The passages used for standardized tests can be boring and seem difficult. Test writers don't use interesting passages or ones that talk about things most people are familiar with. Despite these obstacles, all passages and paragraphs will have the information you need to answer the questions.

The topic of a passage or paragraph is its subject. It's the general idea and can be summed up in a word or short phrase. Sometimes, there is a short description of the passage if it's taken from a longer work. Make sure you read the description as it might state the topic of the passage. If not, read the passage and ask yourself, "Who or what is this about?" For example:

> Over the years, school uniforms have been hotly debated. Arguments are made that students have the right to show individuality and express

themselves by choosing their own clothes. However, this brings up social and academic issues. Some kids cannot afford to wear the clothes they like and might be bullied by the "better dressed" students. With attention drawn to clothes and the individual, students will lose focus on class work and the reason they are in school. School uniforms should be mandatory.

Ask: What is this paragraph about?
Topic: school uniforms

Once you have the topic, it's easier to find the main idea. The main idea is a specific statement telling what the writer wants you to know. Writers usually state the main idea in the form of a thesis statement. If you're looking for the main idea of a single paragraph, the main idea is called the topic sentence and will probably be the first or last sentence. If you're looking for the main idea of an entire passage, look for the thesis statement in either the first or last paragraph. The main idea is usually restated in the conclusion. To find the main idea of a passage or paragraph, follow these steps:

 1. Find the topic.

 2. Ask yourself, "What point is the author trying to make about the topic?"

 3. Create your own sentence summarizing the author's point.

 4. Look in the text for the sentence closest in meaning to yours.

Look at the example paragraph again. It's already established that the topic of the paragraph is school uniforms. What is the main idea/topic sentence?

Ask: "What point is the author trying to make about school uniforms?"

Summary: Students should wear school uniforms.

Topic sentence: School uniforms should be mandatory.
Main Idea: School uniforms should be mandatory.

Each paragraph offers supporting details to explain the main idea. The details could be facts or reasons, but they will always answer a question about the main idea. What? Where? Why? When? How? How much/many? Look at the example paragraph again. You'll notice that more than one sentence answers a question about the main idea. These are the supporting details.

Main Idea: School uniforms should be mandatory.

Ask: Why?

> *Some kids cannot afford to wear clothes they like and could be bullied by the "better dressed" kids.
> **Supporting Detail**
>
> *With attention drawn to clothes and the individual, Students will lose focus on class work and the reason they are in school.
> **Supporting Detail**

What if the author doesn't state the main idea in a topic sentence? The passage will have an implied main idea. It's not as difficult to find as it might seem. Paragraphs are always organized around ideas. To find an implied main idea, you need to know the topic and then find the relationship between the supporting details. Ask yourself, "What is the point the author is making about the relationship between the details?"

> Cocoa is what makes chocolate good for you. Chocolate comes in many varieties. These delectable flavors include milk chocolate, dark chocolate, semi-sweet, and white chocolate.

Ask: What is this paragraph about?
Topic: Chocolate

Ask: What? Where? Why? When? How? How much/many?

Supporting details: Chocolate is good for you because it is made of cocoa, Chocolate is delicious, Chocolate comes in different delicious flavors

Ask: What is the relationship between the details and what is the author's point?

Main Idea: Chocolate is good because it is healthy and it tastes good.

Testing Tips for Main Idea Questions

1. Skim the questions – not the answer choices - before reading the passage.

2. Questions about main idea might use the words "theme," "generalization," or "purpose."

3. Save questions about the main idea for last. Questions can often be found in order in the passage.

3. Underline topic sentences in the passage. Most tests allow you to write in your test booklet.

4. Answer the question in your own words before looking at the answer choices. Then match your answer with an answer choice.

5. Cross out incorrect choices immediately to prevent confusion.

6. If two of the choices mean the same thing but use different words, they are BOTH incorrect.

7. If a question asks about the whole passage, cross out the choices that apply only to part of it.

8. If only part of the information is correct, that choice is incorrect.

9. An choice that is too broad is incorrect. All information needs to be backed up by the passage.

10. Choices with extreme wording are usually incorrect.

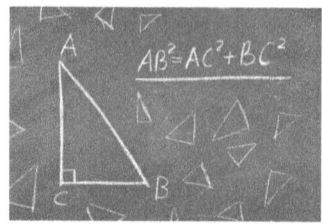

Computational Mathematics

This section contains a self-assessment and math tutorials. The tutorials are designed to familiarize general principles and the self-assessment contains general questions similar to the math questions likely to be on the TABE® exam, but are not intended to be identical to the exam questions. The tutorials are not designed to be a complete math course, and it is assumed that students have some familiarity with math. If you do not understand parts of the tutorial, or find the tutorial difficult, it is recommended that you seek out additional instruction.

Tour of the TABE® Mathematics Content

The TABE® computational mathematics section has 25 questions. Below is a detailed list of the topics likely to appear on the TABE®.

- Convert decimals, percent and fractions

- Calculate percent

- Operations using fractions, percent and fractions

- Basic Algebra

The questions in the self-assessment are not the same as you will find on the TABE® - that would be too easy! And nobody knows what the questions will be and they change all the time. Mostly, the changes consist of substituting new questions for old, but the changes also can be new question formats or styles, changes to the number of questions in each section, changes to the time limits for each section, and combining sections. So, while the format and exact wording of the questions may differ slightly, and changes from year to year, if you can answer the questions below, you will have no problem with the computational mathematics section of the TABE®.

Mathematics Self-Assessment

The purpose of the self-assessment is:

- Identify your strengths and weaknesses.

- Develop your personalized study plan (above)

- Get accustomed to the TABE® format

- Extra practice – the self-assessments are almost a full 3rd practice test!

- Provide a baseline score for preparing your study schedule.

Since this is a Self-assessment, and depending on how confident you are with mathematics, timing yourself is optional. The TABE® has 25 questions, to be answered in 15 minutes, so you have less than a minute for each question. Keep this in mind when managing your time. Some questions you will be able to do very quickly, say, in thirty seconds, and others will take more than a minute.

This self-assessment has 30 questions, so allow about 20 minutes to complete.

Once complete, use the table below to assess your understanding of the content, and prepare your study schedule described in chapter 1.

80% - 100%	Excellent – you have mastered the content
60 – 79%	Good. You have a working knowledge. Even though you can just pass this section, you may want to review the Tutorials and do some extra practice to see if you can improve your mark.
40% - 59%	Below Average. You do not understand the computational math content. Review the tutorials, and retake this quiz again in a few days, before proceeding to the rest of the practice test questions.
Less than 40%	Poor. You have a very limited understanding of computational math. Please review the Tutorials, and retake this quiz again in a few days, before proceeding to the practice test questions.

Answer Sheet

	A	B	C	D	E		A	B	C	D	E
1	○	○	○	○	○	21	○	○	○	○	○
2	○	○	○	○	○	22	○	○	○	○	○
3	○	○	○	○	○	23	○	○	○	○	○
4	○	○	○	○	○	24	○	○	○	○	○
5	○	○	○	○	○	25	○	○	○	○	○
6	○	○	○	○	○	26	○	○	○	○	○
7	○	○	○	○	○	27	○	○	○	○	○
8	○	○	○	○	○	28	○	○	○	○	○
9	○	○	○	○	○	29	○	○	○	○	○
10	○	○	○	○	○	30	○	○	○	○	○
11	○	○	○	○	○						
12	○	○	○	○	○						
13	○	○	○	○	○						
14	○	○	○	○	○						
15	○	○	○	○	○						
16	○	○	○	○	○						
17	○	○	○	○	○						
18	○	○	○	○	○						
19	○	○	○	○	○						
20	○	○	○	○	○						

Math Self-Assessment

Decimals, Fractions and Percent

1. 15 is what percent of 200?

    a. 7.50%
    b. 15%
    c. 20%
    d. 17.50%

2. A boy has 5 red balls, 3 white balls and 2 yellow balls. What percent of the balls are yellow?

    a. 2%
    b. 8%
    c. 20%
    d. 12%

3. Add 10% of 300 to 50% of 20

    a. 50%
    b. 40%
    c. 60%
    d. 45%

4. Convert 75% to a fraction.

    a. 2/100
    b. 85/100
    c. 3/4
    d. 4/7

5. Convert 90% to a fraction

   a. 1/10
   b. 9/9
   c. 10/100
   d. 9/10

6. Multiply 3 by 25% of 40

   a. 75
   b. 30
   c. 68
   d. 35

7. Convert 0.28 to a fraction.

   a. 7/25
   b. 3.25
   c. 8/25
   d. 5/28

8. Convert 0.45 to a fraction

   a. 7/20
   b. 7/45
   c. 9/20
   d. 3/20

9. Convert 1/5 to percent.

   a. 10%
   b. 5%
   c. 20%
   d. 25%

10. Convert 4/20 to percent

   a. 25%
   b. 20%
   c. 40%
   d. 30%

11. A man buys an item for $420 and has a balance of 3000.00. How much did he have before?

   a. $2,580
   b. $3,420
   c. $2,420
   d. $342

12. Divide 9.60 by 3.2

   a. 2.50
   b. 3
   c. 2.3
   d. 6.4

13. If X = 7 solve 3x + 5 − 2x

   a. x = 6
   b. x = 12
   c. x = 1
   d. x = 0

14. 389 + 454 =

   a. 853
   b. 833
   c. 843
   d. 863

15. 9,177 + 7,204 =

   a. 16,471
   b. 16,371
   c. 16,381
   d. 15,412

16. Find the solution to this inequality x + 3 > 12

   a. x < 9
   b. x > 9
   c. x = 9
   d. x = 10

17. Estimate 5205 / 25

   a. 108
   b. 308
   c. 208
   d. 408

Exponents

18. Express in 3^4 standard form

   a. 81
   b. 27
   c. 12
   d. 9

19. Simplify $4^3 + 2^4$

   a. 45
   b. 108
   c. 80
   d. 48

20. If a = 2 and y = 5, solve xy³ - x³

   a. 240
   b. 258
   c. 248
   d. 242

21. X³ x X²

   a. 5ˣ
   b. x⁻⁵
   c. x⁻¹
   d. X⁵

22. Express 100000⁰ standard form

   a. 1
   b. 0
   c. 100000
   d. 1000

23. Solve √144

   a. 14
   b. 72
   c. 24
   d. 12

24. Solve 2/3 + 5/12

   a. 9/17
   b. 3/11
   c. 7/12
   d. 1 1/12

25. 4/5 – 2/5

    a. 2/2
    b. 2/13
    c. 1
    d. 2/15

26. 15/16 x 8/9

    a. 5/6
    b. 16/37
    c. 2/11
    d. 5/7

27. 5/8 ÷ 2/3

    a. 15/16
    b. 10/24
    c. 5/12
    d. 1 2/5

28. 7.25 x 0.5

    a. 3.625
    b. 3.526
    c. 36.25
    d. 35.25

29. 31.5 ÷ 3.5

    a. 8
    b. 9
    c. 8.3
    d. 11.033

30. 7.023 + 2.01

    a. 9.033
    b. 90.33
    c. 73.03
    d. 91.33

Answer Key

1. A
15/200 = X/100 = 1500 = 200X = 15 = 2X = 7.5%

2. C
Total no. of balls = 10, no. of yellow balls = 2, answer = 2/10 X 100 = 20%

3. B
10% of 300 = 30 and 50% of 20 = 10 so 30 + 10 = 40.

4. C
75% = 75/100 = 3/4

5. D
90% = 90/100 = 9/10

6. B
25% of 40 = 10 and 10 x 3 = 30

7. A
0.28 = 28/100 = 7/25

8. C
0.45 = 45/100 = 9/20

9. C
1/5 X 100 = 20%

10. B
4/20 X 100 = 1/5 X 100 = 20%

11. B
(Amount Spent) $420 + $3000 (Balance) = $3,420

12. B
9.60/3.2 = 3

13. B
X=7, so 3x = 3 x 7 = 21, 2x = 2 x 7 = 14, so 21 + 5 - 14 =

26 - 14 = 12. Be careful, to perform the operations in the correct order - multiplication first, then addition and subtraction.

14. C
389 + 454 = 843

15. C
9,177 + 7,204 = 16,381

16. B
X > 12 − 3, = x > 9

17. C
The approximate answer to 5205 / 25 is 208. The actual answer is 208.2

18. A
3 x 3 x 3 x 3 = 81

19. C
(4 x 4 x 4) + (2 x 2 x 2 x 2) = 64 + 16 = 80

20. D
$2(5)^3 - (2)^3 = 2(125) - 8 = 250 - 8 = 242$

21. D
$X^3 \times X^2 = X^{3+2} = X^5$

22. A
Any value (except 0) raised to the power of 0 equals 1.

23. D
$\sqrt{144} = 12$

24. D
A common denominator is needed, a number which both 3 and 12 will divide into. So, 8+5/12 = 13/12 = 1 1/12

25. D
A common denominator is needed, a number which both 5 and 3 will divide into. So 12-10/15 = 2/15

26. A
Since there are common numerators and denominators to cancel out, we cancel out 15/16 x 8/9 to get 5/2 x 1/3, and then multiply numerators and denominators to get 5/6.

27. A
To divide fractions, we multiply the first fraction with the inverse of the second fraction. Therefore we have 5/8 x 3/2, = 15/16

28. A
7.25 x 0.5 = 3.625

29. B
31.5 ÷ 3.5 = 9

30. A
7.023 + 2.01 = 9.033

Basic Math Video Tutorials

Visit us Online for the video version of these tutorials

https://www.test-preparation.ca/basic-math-video-tutorials/

Fraction Tips, Tricks and Shortcuts

When you are writing an exam, time is precious, so anything you can do to answer questions faster is a real advantage.

Here are some ideas, shortcuts, tips and tricks that can speed up answering fraction problems.

Remember that a fraction is just a number which names a portion of something. For instance, instead of having a whole pie, a fraction says you have a part of a pie--such as a half of one or a fourth of one.

Two numbers make up a fraction. The number on top is the numerator. The number on the bottom is the denominator.

To remember which is which, just remember that "denominator" and "down" both start with a "d." And the "downstairs" number is the denominator. So for instance, in ½, the numerator is 1, and the denominator (or "downstairs") number is 2.

Adding Fractions

It's easy to add two fractions if they have the same denominator. Just add the digits on top and leave the bottom one the same: 1/10 + 6/10 = 7/10.

It's the same with subtracting fractions with the same denominator: 7/10 - 6/10 = 1/10.

Adding and subtracting fractions with different denominators is a little more complicated.

First, you have to arrange the fractions so they have the same denominators.

The easiest way to do this is to multiply the denominators: For 2/5 + 1/2 multiply 5 by 2. Now you have a denominator of 10.

But now you have to change the top numbers too. Since you multiplied the 5 in 2/5 by 2, you also multiply the 2 by 2, to get 4. So the first fraction is now 4/10.

In the second fraction, you multiplied the denominator by 5, you have to multiply the numerator by 5 also, to get 5/10.

Now you have 4/10 + 5/10 and you can add 5 and 4 to get 9/10.

Simplest Form

To reduce a fraction to its simplest form, you have to arrange the numerator and denominator so the only common factor is 1.

Think of it this way:

Let's take an example: The fraction 2/10.

This is not reduced to its simplest terms because there is a number that will divide evenly into both: 2. We want to make it so that the only number that will divide evenly into both is 1.

Divide the top and bottom by 2 to get the new, reduced fraction - 1/5.

Multiplying Fractions

This is the easiest of all: Just multiply the two top numbers and then multiply the two bottom numbers.

Here is an example,

2/5 X 2/3

First, multiply the numerators: 2 X 2 = 4

then multiply the denominators: 5 X 3 = 15

Your answer is 4/15.

Dividing Fractions

Dividing fractions is easy if you remember a simple trick - first turn the second fraction upside down - then multiply!

Here is an example:

7/8 X 1/2

Turn the second fraction upside down:

7/8 X 2/1

then multiply:

(7 X 2) / (8 X 1) = 14/8

CONVERTING FRACTIONS TO DECIMALS

There are a couple of ways to convert fractions to decimals. The first, which is the fastest -- is to memorize some basic fraction facts.

1/100 is "one hundredth," expressed as a decimal, it's .01.

> 1/50 is "two hundredths," expressed as a decimal, it's .02.
>
> 1/25 is "one twenty-fifth" or "four hundredths," expressed as a decimal, it's .04.
>
> 1/20 is "one twentieth" or ""five hundredths," expressed as a decimal, it's .05.
>
> 1/10 is "one tenth," expressed as a decimal, it's .1.
>
> 1/8 is "one eighth," or "one hundred twenty-five thousandths," expressed as a decimal, it's .125.
>
> 1/5 is "one fifth," or "two tenths," expressed as a decimal, it's .2.
>
> 1/4 is "one fourth" or "twenty-five hundredths," expressed as a decimal, it's .25.
>
> 1/3 is "one third" or "thirty-three hundredths," expressed as a decimal, it's .33.
>
> 1/2 is "one half" or "five tenths," expressed as a decimal, it's .5.
>
> 3/4 is "three fourths," or "seventy-five hundredths," expressed as a decimal, it's .75.

Of course, if you're no good at memorization, another good technique for converting a fraction to a decimal is to manipulate it so that the fraction's denominator is 10, 100, 1000, or some other power of 10.

Here's an example: We'll start with three quarters. What is the first number in the 4 "times table" that you can multiply and get a multiple of 10? Can you multiply 4 by something to get 10? No. Can you multiply it by something to get 100? Yes! 4 X 25 is 100.

So multiply the numerator by 25, which is 75 over 100

We know fractions are really a division problem, and we also know that dividing by 100, means we move the decimal 2 places to the left.

So, 75 over 100 = .75

Lets try another example - Convert one fifth to a decimal.

First find a power of 10 that 5 goes into evenly, which is 2.

Multiply the numerator and denominator by 2, which is

2/10.

Dividing 2 by 10 means we move the decimal place 1 place to the left.

So one fifth = 0.2

Converting Fractions to Percent

Here is a quick method to convert fraction to percent and a strategy for answering on a multiple choice test that will save you valuable exam time.

First, remember that a fraction is a division problem: you're dividing the bottom number into the top.

Taking an example, convert 2/3 into percent.

The first method is to multiple the numerator by 100 and divide. So,

(2 X 100) / 2 = 100/3 = 66.66

Add a % sign and you have the answer, 66.66%

If you're doing these conversions on a multiple-choice test, here's an idea that might be even easier and faster. Let's say you have a fraction of 1/8 and you're asked to convert to percent.

Since we know that "percent" means hundredths, ask yourself what number we can multiply 8 by to get 100. Since there is no number, ask what number gets us close to 100.

That number is 12: 8 X 12 = 96. So it gets us a little less than 100. Now, whatever you do to the denominator, you have to do to the numerator. Let's multiply 1 X 12 and we get 12. However, since 96 is a little less than 100, we know that our answer will be a little MORE than 12%.

Look at the choices and eliminate the obvious wrong choices. So if your possible answers on the multiple-choice test are these:

a) 8.5% b) 19% c) 12.5% d) 25%

then we know the answer is c) 12.5%, because it's a little MORE than the 12 we got in our math problem above.

Here all the choices except choice C 12.5% can be eliminated.

You don't have to know the exact correct answer, just enough to estimate, then eliminate the obviously wrong answers.

This was an easy example to demonstrate the strategy, but don't be fooled! You probably won't get such an easy question on your exam. By estimating your answer quickly, then eliminating obviously incorrect choices immediately, you save precious exam time.

Decimal Tips, Tricks and Shortcuts

Converting Decimals to Fractions

Converting decimals to fractions is easy if you say it the right way! If you say "point one" or "point 25", you'll have trouble.

But if you say, "one tenth" and "twenty-five hundredths," then you have already solved it! That's because, if you know your fractions, you know that "one tenth" looks like this: 1/10. And "twenty-five hundredths" looks like this: 25/100.

Even if you have digits before the decimal, such as 3.4, learning how to say the word will help you with the conversion into a fraction. It's not "three point four," it's "three and four tenths." Knowing this, you know that the fraction which looks like "three and four tenths" is 3 4/10.

The conversion is not complete until you reduce the fraction to its lowest terms: It's not 25/100, but 1/4.

Converting Decimals to Percent

Changing a decimal to a percent is easy if you remember one thing: multiply by 100.

For example, if you start with .45, simply multiply it by 100 for 45. Then add the % sign to the end - 45%.

Think of it this way: take out the decimal point, add a percent sign on the opposite side. In other words, the decimal on the left is replaced by the % on the right.

It doesn't work quite that easily if the decimal is in the middle of the number. For example, 3.7. Here, take out the decimal in the middle and replace it with a 0 % at the end. So 3.7 converted to decimal is 370%.

Percent Tips, Tricks and Shortcuts

Percent problems are not nearly as scary as they appear, if you remember this neat trick:

Draw a cross as in:

Portion	Percent
Whole	100

In the upper left, write PORTION. In the bottom left write WHOLE. In the top right, write PERCENT and in the bottom right, write 100. Whatever your problem is, you will leave blank the unknown, and fill in the other four parts. For example, let's suppose your problem is: Find 10% of 50. Since we know the 10% part, we put 10 in the percent corner. Since the whole number in our problem is 50, we put that in the corner marked whole. You always put 100 underneath the percent, so we leave it as is, which leaves only the top left corner blank. This is where we'll put our answer. Now simply multiply the two corner numbers that are NOT 100. In this case, it's 10 X 50. That gives us 500. Now divide this by the remaining corner, or 100, to get a final answer of 5. 5 is the number that goes in the upper-left corner, and is your final solution.

Another hint to remember: Percents are the same thing as hundredths in decimals. So .45 is the same as 45 hundredths or 45 percent.

Converting Percents to Decimals

Percents are just a type of decimal, so it should be no surprise that converting between the two is actually fairly simple. Here are a few tricks and shortcuts to keep in mind:

- ☐ Remember that percent literally means "per 100" or "for every 100." So when you speak of 30% you're

saying 30 for every 100 or the fraction 30/100. In basic math, you learned that fractions that have 10 or 100 as the denominator can easily be turned to a decimal. 30/100 is thirty hundredths, or expressed as a decimal, .30.
- Another way to look at it: To convert a percent to a decimal, simply divide the number by 100. So for instance, if the percent is 47%, divide 47 by 100. The result will be .47. Get rid of the % mark and you're done.
- Remember that the easiest way of dividing by 100 is by moving your decimal two spots to the left.

Converting Percents to Fractions

Converting percents to fractions is easy. After all, a percent is just a type of fraction; it tells you what part of 100 that you're talking about. Here are some simple ideas for making the conversion from a percent to a fraction:

- If the percent is a whole number -- say 34% -- then simply write a fraction with 100 as the denominator (the bottom number). Then put the percentage itself on top. So 34% becomes 34/100.
- Now reduce as you would reduce any percent. Here, by dividing 2 into 34 and 2 into 100, you get 17/50.
- If your percent is not a whole number -- say 3.4% --then convert it to a decimal expressed as hundredths. 3.4 is the same as 3.40 (or 3 and forty hundredths). Now ask yourself how you would express "three and forty hundredths" as a fraction. It would, of course, be 3 40/100. Reduce this and it becomes 3 2/5.

Exponents: Tips, Shortcuts & Tricks

Exponents are just shorthand for saying that you're multiplying a number by itself two or more times.

For instance, instead of saying 5 x 5 x 5, you can show that you're multiplying 5 by itself 3 times if you just write 5^3.

We usually say this as "five to the third power" or "five to the power of three." In this example, the raised 3 is an "exponent," and the 5 is the "base."

You can even use exponents with fractions. For instance, $1/2^3$ means you're multiplying 1/2 x 1/2 x 1/2. (The answer is 1/8).

Multiplying Exponents

For exponents with the same base, for instance 5^3 X 5^2, add the exponents on the same base. The answer, then, is 5^5.

If the bases are different, for example, in 5^3 X 3^2, you have to do the math the long way to figure it out.

5 x 5 x 5 = 125, and 3 X 3 = 9.

125 X 9 = 1125

Dividing Exponents

For exponents with the same base, subtract the exponents. In the problem above, 5^3 X 5^2, 3 - 2 = 1. 5 to the power of 1 is 5.

Here are some Quick things to remember

Any number to the power of 1 is that number.

Any number raised to the power of 0 is 1.

Number (x)	X^2	X^3
1	1	1
2	4	8
3	9	27
4	16	64
5	25	125
6	36	216
7	49	343
8	64	512
9	81	729
10	100	1000

How to Answer Basic Math Multiple Choice

The time allowed on the math portion of a standardized test is typically so short that there's no room for error. You have to be fast and accurate.

Math strategy is very helpful, but nothing beats knowing your stuff! Make sure that you have learned all the important formulas that will be used.

If you don't know the formulas, strategy won't help you.

How to Answer Basic Math Questions - the Basics

First, read the problem, but not the answers.

Work through the problem first and come up with your own answers. Hopefully, you should find your answer among the choices.

If no answer matches the one you got, re-check your math, but this time, use a different method. In math, there are different ways to solve a problem.

Math Multiple Choice Strategy

The two strategies for working with basic math multiple choice are Estimation and Elimination.

Estimation is just as it sounds - try to estimate an approximate answer first. Then look at the choices.

Elimination is probably the most powerful strategy for answering multiple choice.

Eliminate obviously incorrect answers and narrowing the possible choices.

Here are a few basic math examples of how this works.

Solve 2/3 + 5/12

    a. 9/17

    b. 3/11

    c. 7/12

    d. 1 1/12

First estimate the answer. 2/3 is more than half and 5/12 is about half, so the answer is going to be very close to 1.

Next, Eliminate. Choice A is about 1/2 and can be eliminated, choice B is very small, less than 1/2 and can be eliminated. Choice C is close to 1/2 and can be eliminated. Leaving only choice D, which is just over 1.

Work through the solution, find a common denominator and add. The correct answer is 1 1/12, so Choice D is correct.

Let's look at another example:

Solve 4/5 – 2/3

    a. 2/2
    b. 2/13
    c. 1
    d. 2/15

First, quickly estimate the answer. 4/5 is very close to 1, and 2/3 more than half, so the answer is going to be less than 1/2.

Choice A can be eliminated right away, because it is 1. Choice C can be eliminated for the same reason.

Next, look at the denominators. Since 5 and 3 don't go into 13, choice B can be eliminated as well.

That leaves choice D. Checking the answer, the common denominator will be 15. So the answer is 2/15 and choice D is correct.

Fractions shortcut - Cancelling out.

In any operation with fractions, if the numerator of one fractions has a common multiple with the denominator of the other, you can cancel out. This saves time, and simplifies the problem quickly, making it easier to manage.

Solve 2/15 ÷ 4/5

    a. 6/65

    b. 6/75

    c. 5/12

    d. 1/6

To divide fractions, we multiply the first fraction with the inverse of the second fraction. Therefore we have 2/15 x 5/4. The numerator of the first fraction, 2, shares a multiple with the denominator of the second fraction, 4, which is 2. These cancel out, which gives, 1/3 x 1/2 = 1/6

Cancelling Out solved the questions very quickly, but we can still use multiple choice strategies to answer.

Choice B can be eliminated because 75 is too large a denominator. Choice C can be eliminated because 5 and 15 don't go into 12.

Choice D is correct.

Decimal Multiple Choice Strategy and Shortcuts.

Multiplying decimals gives a very quick way to estimate and eliminate choices. Anytime that you multiply decimals, it is going to give a answer with the same number of decimal places as the combined operands.

So for example,

2.38 X 1.2 will produce a number with three places of decimal, which is 2.856.

Here are a few examples with step-by-step explanation:

Solve 2.06 x 1.2

    a. 24.82

    b. 2.482

    c. 24.72

    d. 2.472

This is a simple question, but even before you start calculating, you can eliminate several choices. When multiplying decimals, there will always be as many numbers behind the decimal place in the answer as the sum of the ones in the initial problem, so choices A and C can be eliminate.

The correct answer is D: 2.06 x 1.2 = 2.472

Solve 20.0 ÷ 2.5

    a. 12.05

    b. 9.25

    c. 8.3

    d. 8

First estimate the answer to be around 10, and eliminate choice A. And since it'd also be an even number, you can eliminate Choices B and C, leaving only choice D.

The correct answer is D: 20.0 ÷ 2.5 = 8

Order Of Operation

Some math calculations contain more than one set of operations. For example, a problem like 3 + (35 - 21) x 2 requires addition, subtraction and multiplication operations. The problem arises from the confusion of which of the operations to perform first. Starting with the wrong operation will give you the wrong answer. To solve this dilemma and to avoid confusion, the Order of Operation rules were set.

Order of operation is a set of mathematical rules designed to be used for calculations that require more than one arithmetic operation. For example, calculation problems that require two or more out of addition, subtraction, multiplication and division, would require that you follow the order of operation to solve.

The order of operation rules are quite simple as explained below.

> **Rule 1:** Start with calculations that are inside brackets or parentheses.
> **Rule 2:** Then, solve all multiplications and divisions, from left to right.
> **Rule 3:** Finally, solve all additions and subtractions, from left to right.

Example 1

Solve 16 + 5 x 8
Based on the rules above, we would have to start with the multiplication part of the question.
That will give: 16 + 40 = 56

Take note that if the rule was not followed and addition was done first, the answer gotten would be different and wrong.

16 + 5 x 8
21 x 8 = 168 (wrong answer)

Example 2

3 +(35 - 21) x 2

Based on the rules of the order of operation, we have to solve the problem in the bracket or parenthesis first. Then we do the multiplication, before doing the addition.

3 + (35 - 21) x 2
3 + (14) x 3
3 + 42
= 45

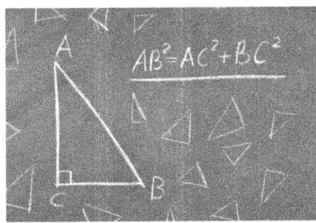

Applied Mathematics

THIS SECTION CONTAINS A SELF-ASSESSMENT AND APPLIED MATHEMATICS TUTORIALS. The tutorials are designed to familiarize general principles and the self-assessment contains general questions similar to the applied math questions likely to be on the TABE® exam, but are not intended to be identical to the exam questions. The tutorials are not designed to be a complete applied math course, and it is assumed that students have some familiarity with applied math. If you do not understand parts of the tutorial, or find the tutorial difficult, it is recommended that you seek out additional instruction.

Tour of the TABE® Applied Mathematics Content

The TABE® applied mathematics section has 25 questions. Below is a detailed list of the mathematics topics likely to appear on the TABE®. Make sure that you understand these topics at the very minimum.

- Solve word problems based on the computational math content areas

- Interpreting graphs

- Basic geometry

The questions in the self-assessment are not the same as you will find on the TABE® - that would be too easy! And nobody knows what the questions will be and they change all the time. Mostly, the changes consist of substituting new questions for old, but the changes also can be new question formats or styles, changes to the number of questions in each section, changes to the time limits for each section, and combining sections. So, while the format and exact wording of the questions may differ slightly, and changes from year to year, if you can answer the questions below, you will have no problem with the mathematics section of the TABE®.

Applied Mathematics Self-Assessment

The purpose of the self-assessment is:

- Identify your strengths and weaknesses.
- Develop your personalized study plan (above)
- Get accustomed to the TABE® format
- Extra practice – the self-assessments are almost a full 3rd practice test!
- Provide a baseline score for preparing your study schedule.

Since this is a self-assessment, and depending on how confident you are with applied mathematics, timing yourself is optional. The TABE® has 25 questions, to be answered in 25 minutes. This self-assessment has 20 questions, so allow about 20 minutes to complete.

Once complete, use the table below to assess your understanding of the content, and prepare your study schedule described in chapter 1.

80% - 100%	Excellent – you have mastered the content
60 – 79%	Good. You have a working knowledge. Even though you can just pass this section, you may want to review the Tutorials and do some extra practice to see if you can improve your mark.
40% - 59%	Below Average. You do not understand the applied math content. Review the tutorials, and retake this quiz again in a few days, before proceeding to the rest of the practice test questions.
Less than 40%	Poor. You have a very limited understanding of applied math. Please review the Tutorials, and retake this quiz again in a few days, before proceeding to the practice test questions.

Applied Math Answer Sheet

	A	B	C	D
1	○	○	○	○
2	○	○	○	○
3	○	○	○	○
4	○	○	○	○
5	○	○	○	○
6	○	○	○	○
7	○	○	○	○
8	○	○	○	○
9	○	○	○	○
10	○	○	○	○
11	○	○	○	○
12	○	○	○	○
13	○	○	○	○
14	○	○	○	○
15	○	○	○	○
16	○	○	○	○
17	○	○	○	○
18	○	○	○	○
19	○	○	○	○
20	○	○	○	○

Applied Mathematics 69

1. The total expense of building a fence around a square-shaped field is $2000 at a rate of $5 per meter. What is the length of one side?

   a. 80 meters
   b. 100 meters
   c. 40 meters
   d. 320 meters

2. There are some oranges in a basket. By adding 8/5 of the total to the basket the new total became 130. How many oranges were in the basket?

   a. 50
   b. 60
   c. 40
   d. 35

3. Write 41.061 to the nearest 10th.

   a. 41.1
   b. 41.06
   c. 41
   d. 41.6

4. The following numbers represent the ages of people on a bus – 3, 6, 27, 13, 6, 8, 12, 20, 5, 10. Calculate their mean of their ages.

   a. 11
   b. 6
   c. 9
   d. 110

5. A square-shaped lawn has an area of 62,500 square meters. What is the cost of building fence around it at a rate of $5.5 per meter?

    a. $4,000
    b. $5,500
    c. $4,500
    d. $5,000

6. A building is 15 m long and 20 m wide and 10 m high. What is the volume of the building?

    a 45 m³
    b. 3,000 m³
    c. 1500 m³
    d. 300 m³

7. Mr. Brown bought 5 cheese burgers, 3 drinks and 4 orders of fries for his family and a cookie pack for his dog. If the price of all single items is same at $1.30, and a 3.5% tax is added, what is the total cost of dinner?

    a. $17.00
    b. $16.90
    c. $17.49
    d. $16.00

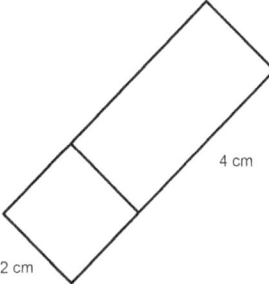

Note: Figure not drawn to scale.

8. Assuming the shape with a 2 cm side is square, what is the perimeter of the above shape?

    a. 12 cm
    b. 16 cm
    c. 6 cm
    d. 20 cm

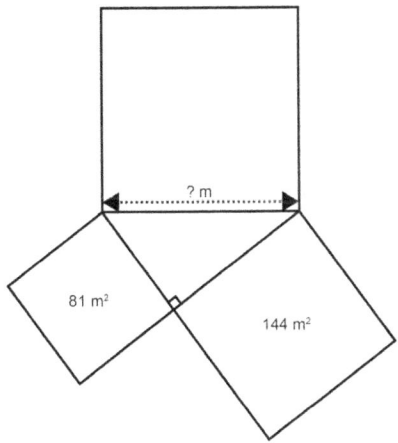

Note: Figure not drawn to scale.

9. Assuming the shapes around the right triangle above are square, what is the length of each side of the indicated square above?

   a. 10
   b. 15
   c. 20
   d. 5

10. A bag contains 38 black balls and 42 white balls. What is the ratio of black balls to white?

   a. 9:11
   b. 1:3
   c. 19:21
   d. 11:9

11. 3 boys are asked to clean a surface that is 4 ft². If the portion is divided equally among the boys, what size will each of them clean?

   a. 1 ft 6 inches²
   b. 14 inches²
   c. 1 ft 2 inches²
   d. . 1 ft² 48 inches²

12. Consider the following population growth chart.

Country	Population 2000	Population 2005
Japan	122,251,000	128,057,000
China	1,145,195,000	1,341,335,000
United States	253,339,000	310,384,000
Indonesia	184,346,000	239,871,000

Which country is growing the fastest?

    a. Japan

    b. China

    c. United States

    d. Indonesia

13. Translate the following into an equation: six times a number plus five.

    a. 6X + 5

    b. 6(X+5)

    c. 5X + 6

    d. (6 * 5) + 5

14. A small business owner deposits $6000 in a savings account at a local bank. After 2 years, at 3% interest rate, what will be the interest earned?

    a. $6360

    b. $360

    c. $240

    d. $460

15. Adelle is making spaghetti. The recipe says that for 500 grams of spaghetti, she should add 0.75 grams of salt. However, she just wants 125 grams of spaghetti. Based on this information, how much salt should she use?

    a. 0.38 grams

    b. 0.75 grams

    c. 0.19 grams

    d. 0.25 grams

16. A pet store sold $19,304.56 worth of merchandise in June. If the cost of products sold was $5,284.34, employees were paid $8,384.76, and rent was $2,920.00, how much profit did the store make in June?

    a. $5,635.46
    b. $2,715.46
    c. $14,020.22
    d. $10,019.80

17. A caterer is hired for a wedding and must calculate how much wine is required. The wedding couple gets two liters of wine and each guest receives 0.20 liters. If y is the total number of liters required, and x is the number of wedding guests, which equation below should be used?

    a. $y = 0.20x + 2$
    b. $y = 2x + 0.20$
    c. $y = 2.20x$
    d. $x = 0.20y + 2$

18. If 144 students would like to hire buses for a ski trip. How many buses will be required if each bus carries 36 students?

    a. 6
    b. 5
    c. 4
    d. 3

19. The cost of waterproofing canvas is .50 a square yard. What's the total cost for waterproofing a canvas truck cover if the size is 15' x 24'?

    a. $18.00

    b. $6.67

    c. $180.00

    d. $20.00

20. If a square if five feet tall, what is the volume?

    a. 5 feet^3

    b. 100 feet^3

    c. 25 feet^3

    d. 125 feet^3

Answer Key

1. B
Total expense is $2000 and we are informed that $5 is spent per meter. Combining these two information, we know that the total length of the fence is 2000/5 = 400 meters.

The fence is built around a square-shaped field. If one side of the square is "a," the perimeter of the square is "4a." Here, the perimeter is equal to 400 meters. So,

400 = 4a

100 = a → this means that one side of the square is equal to 100 meters

2. A
Suppose oranges in the basket before = x
Then: X + 8x/5 = 130
5x + 8x = 650 (multiply both sides by 5)
13x = 650, x = 650/13
X = 50

3. A
The number is 41.061. The last digit 1, which is less than 5, and so it's discarded. The next digit, 6, is greater than 5 and so is removed and 1 is added to the next digit to the left. Answer = 41.1

4. A
First add all the numbers 3 + 6 + 27 + 13 + 6 + 8 + 12 + 20 + 5 + 10 = 110. Then divide by 10 (the number of data provided) = 110/10 = 11

5. B
As the lawn is square, the length of one side will be = $\sqrt{62,500}$ = 250 meters. So the perimeters will be 250 × 4 = 1000 meters. The total cost will be 1000 × 5.5 = $5500.

6. D
Formula for volume of a shape is L x W x H = 15 x 20 x 10 = 3,000 m³

7. C
The price of all the single items is same and there are 13 items. So the total cost will be 13 X 1.3 = $16.90. After the 3.5% tax, the total will be 16.9 X 1.035 = $17.49.

8. B
We see that there is a square with side 2 cm and a rectangle adjacent to it, with one side 2 cm (common side with the square) and the other side 4 cm. The perimeter of a shape is found by summing up all sides surrounding the shape, not adding the ones inside the shape. Three 2 cm sides from the square, and two 4 cm sides and one 2 cm side from the rectangle contribute the perimeter.

So, the perimeter of the shape is: 2 + 2 + 2 + 4 + 2 + 4 = 16 cm.

9. B
We see that there are three squares forming a right triangle in the middle. Two of the squares have the areas 81 m² and 144 m². If we denote their sides a and b respectively:

a^2 = 81 and b^2 = 144. The length which is asked is the hypotenuse; a and b are the opposite and adjacent sides of the right angle. By using the Pythagorean Theorem, we can find the value of the asked side:

$(Hypotenuse)^2 = (Perpendicular)^2 + (Base)^2$
$h^2 = a^2 + b^2$

$a^2 = 81, b^2 = 144$
$h^2 = a^2 + b^2$
$h^2 = 81+144$
$h^2 = 225$
$h = 15$

10. C
The ratio of black balls to white is 38:42. Reduce to lowest terms = 19:21

11. D
1 foot is equal to 12 inches. So 1 ft² = 12 * 12 in²
4 ft² = 4 * 12 * 12 in² = 576 in²

The total surface area is divided equally among 3 boys.

Each boy will clean 576/3 = 192 in²

192 in² = 144 in² + 48 in²; 144 in² = 1 ft²

So, each boy will clean 1 ft² and 48 in²

12. D
Indonesia is growing the fastest at about 30%.

13. B
Six times a number plus five is the same as saying six times (a number plus five). Or, 6 * (a number plus five). Let X be the number so, 6(X+5).

14. B
Interest (I) = ?, Rate (r) = 3%, Time (t) = 2 years, Principal (P) = 6000. Convert rate to decimal. 3% = 0.03. Then plug in variables into the simple interest formula. I = P x r x t, I = 6000 x 0.03 x 2, I = $360

15. C
125 : 500 is the same as 25 : 100 or 1 : 4. So the amount of salt will be 0.75/4 = 0.1875, or about .19 grams.

16. B
Total expenses = 5284.34 + 8,384.76 + 2,920.00 = 16589.10
Profit = revenue less expenses

$19,304.56 - 16589.10 = 2715.46

17. A
The equation to calculate the total number of liters is y = 2 + 0.2x. Notice that you can eliminate choice D right away since the total amount will be equal to y.

18. C
Each bus carries 36 students, and there are 144 students so the number of buses will be 144/36 = 4.

19. D
First calculate total square feet, which is 15 X 24 = 360 sq. ft. Next convert to square yards, (1sq. ft. = 0.1111 sq. yards) which is 360 X 0.1111 = 39.9999 or 40 square yards. At $0.50 per square yard, the total cost is $20.

20. D
Formula for volume of a shape is L x W x H. The square is 5 feet tall, and since all sides are equal, the area will be 5 X 5 X 5 = 125 feet^3.

How to Solve Word Problems

Do you know what the biggest tip for solving word problems is?

Practice regularly and systematically.

Sounds simple and easy right? Yes it is, and yes it really does work.

Word problems are a way of thinking and require you to translate a real-world problem into mathematical terms.

Some math teachers say that learning how to think mathematically is the main reason for teaching word problems.

So what does that mean?

Studying word problems and math in general requires a logical and mathematical frame of mind. The only way you can get this is by practicing regularly, which means every day.

It is critical that you practice word problems every day for the 5 days before the exam as the absolute minimum.

If you practice and miss a day, you have lost the mathematical frame of mind and the benefit of your previous practice is gone. You must start all over again.

Everything is important.

All the information given in the problem has some purpose. There is no unnecessary information! Word problems are typically around 50 words in 2 or 3 sentences.

Often, the relationships are complicated. To explain everything, every word counts.

Make sure that you use every piece of information.

7 steps to solving word problems.

Step 1 — Read through the problem at least three times. The first reading should be a quick scan, and the next two readings should be done slowly to find answers to these questions:

> What does the problem ask? (Usually located at the end)

Mark all information and underline all important words or phrases.

Step 2 – Draw a picture. Use arrows, circles, lines, whatever works for you. This makes the problem real.

A favorite word problem is something like, 1 train leaves Station A travelling at 100 km/hr and another train leaves Station B travelling at 60 km/hr. ...

Draw a line, the two stations, and the two trains at either end.

Depending on the question, make a table with a blank portion to show information you don't know.

Step 3 – Assign a single letter to represent each unknown.

You may want to note the unknown that each letter represents so you don't get confused.

Step 4 – Translate the information into an equation.

Remember that the main problem with word problems is that they are not expressed in regular math equations. Your ability to identify correctly the variables and translate the information into an equation determines your ability to solve the problem.

Step 5 – Check the equation to see if it looks like regular equations that you are used to seeing and whether it looks sensible.

Does the equation appear to represent the information in the question? Take note that you may need to rewrite some formulas needed to solve the word problem equation.

Step 6 – Use algebra rules to solve the equation.

Simplify each side of the equation by removing parentheses and combining like terms.

Use addition or subtraction to isolate the variable term on one side of the equation. If a number crosses to the other side of the equation, the sign changes to the opposite -- for example positive to negative.

Use multiplication or division to solve for the variable. What you to once side of the equation you must do for the other.

Where there are multiple unknowns you will need to use elimination or substitution methods to resolve all the equations.

Step 7 – Check your final answers to see if they make sense with the information given in the problem.

For example, if the word problem involves a discount, the final price should be less or if a product was taxed then the final answer has to cost more.

Types of Word Problems

Word problems can be classified into 12 types. Below are examples of each type with a complete solution. Some types of word problems can be solved quickly using multiple choice strategies and some cannot. Always look for ways to estimate the answer and then eliminate choices.

1. Age

A girl is 10 years older than her brother. By next year, she will be twice the age of her brother. What are their ages now?

    a. 25, 15
    b. 19, 9
    c. 21, 11
    d. 29, 19

Solution: B

We will assume that the girl's age is "a" and her brother's is "b." This means that based on the information in the first sentence,
$a = 10 + b$

Next year, she will be twice her brother's age, which gives
$a + 1 = 2(b + 1)$

We need to solve for one unknown factor and then use the answer to solve for the other. To do this we substitute the value of "a" from the first equation into the second equation. This gives

$10 + b + 1 = 2b + 2$
$11 + b = 2b + 2$
$11 - 2 = 2b - b$
$b = 9$

9 = b this means that her brother is 9 years old. Solving for the girl's age in the first equation gives a = 10 + 9. a = 19 the girl is aged 19. So, the girl is aged 19 and the boy is 9

2. Distance or speed

Two boats travel down a river towards the same destination, starting at the same time. One boat is traveling at 52 km/hr, and the other boat at 43 km/hr. How far apart will they be after 40 minutes?

    a. 46.67 km
    b. 19.23 km
    c. 6.04 km
    d. 14.39 km

Solution: C
After 40 minutes, the first boat will have traveled = 52 km/hr x 40 minutes/60 minutes = 34.7 km
After 40 minutes, the second boat will have traveled = 43 km/hr x 40/60 minutes = 28.66 km
Difference between the two boats will be 34.7 km – 28.66 km = 6.04 km.

Multiple Choice Strategy

First estimate the answer. The first boat is travelling 9 km. faster than the second, for 40 minutes, which is 2/3 of an hour. 2/3 of 9 – 6, as a rough guess of the distance apart.

Choices A, B and D can be eliminated right away.

3. Ratio

The instructions in a cookbook states that 700 grams of flour must be mixed in 100 ml of water, and 0.90 grams of salt added. A cook however has just 325 grams of flour. What is the quantity of water and salt that he should use?

a. 0.41 grams and 46.4 ml
b. 0.45 grams and 49.3 ml
c. 0.39 grams and 39.8 ml
d. 0.25 grams and 40.1 ml

Solution: A

The Cookbook states 700 grams of flour, but the cook only has 325. The first step is to determine the percentage of flour he has 325/700 x 100 = 46.4%
That means that 46.4% of all other items must also be used.
46.4% of 100 = 46.4 ml of water
46.4% of 0.90 = 0.41 grams of salt.

Multiple Choice Strategy

The recipe calls for 700 grams of flour but the cook only has 325, which is just less than half, the amount of water and salt are going to be about half.

Choices C and D can be eliminated right away. Choice B is very close so be careful. Looking closely at choice B, it is exactly half, and since 325 is slightly less than half of 700, it can't be correct.

Choice A is correct.

4. Percent

An agent received $6,685 as his commission for selling a property. If his commission was 13% of the selling price, how much was the property?

a. $68,825
b. $121,850
c. $49,025
d. $51,423

Solution: D

Let's assume that the property price is x
That means from the information given, 13% of x = 6,685
Solve for x,
x = 6685 x 100/13 = $51,423

Multiple Choice Strategy

The commission, 13%, is just over 10%, which is easier to work with. Round up $6685 to $6700, and multiple by 10 for an approximate answer. 10 X 6700 = $67,000. You can do this in your head. Choice B is much too big and can be eliminated. Choice C is too small and can be eliminated. Choices A and D are left and good possibilities.

Do the calculations to make the final choice.

5. Sales & Profit

A store owner buys merchandise for $21,045. He transports them for $3,905 and pays his staff $1,450 to stock the merchandise on his shelves. If he does not incur further costs, how much does he need to sell the items to make $5,000 profit?

   a. $32,500
   b. $29,350
   c. $32,400
   d. $31,400

Solution: D

Total cost of the items is $21,045 + $3,905 + $1,450 = $26,400
Total cost is now $26,400 + $5000 profit = $31,400

Multiple Choice Strategy

Round off and add the numbers up in your head quickly. 21,000 + 4,000 + 1500 = 26500. Add in 5000 profit for a total of 31500.

Choice B is too small and can be eliminated. Choices C and A are too large and can be eliminated.

6. Tax/Income

A woman earns $42,000 per month and pays 5% tax on her monthly income. If the Government increases her monthly taxes by $1,500, what is her income after tax?

   a. $38,400
   b. $36,050
   c. $40,500
   d. $39, 500

Solution: A

Initial tax on income was 5/100 x 42,000 = $2,100
$1,500 was added to the tax to give $2,100 + 1,500 = $3,600
Income after tax left is $42,000 - $3,600 = $38,400

7. Averaging

The average weight of 10 books is 54 grams. 2 more books were added and the average weight became 55.4. If one of the 2 new books added weighed 62.8 g, what is the weight of the other?

   a. 44.7 g
   b. 67.4 g
   c. 62 g
   d. 52 g

Solution: C

Total weight of 10 books with average 54 grams will be = 10 × 54 = 540 g
Total weight of 12 books with average 55.4 will be = 55.4 × 12 = 664.8 g
So total weight of the remaining 2 will be= 664.8 − 540 = 124.8 g
If one weighs 62.8, the weight of the other will be= 124.8 g − 62.8 g = 62 g

Multiple Choice Strategy

Averaging problems can be estimated by looking at which direction the average goes. If additional items are added and the average goes up, the new items much be greater than the average. If the average goes down after new items are added, the new items must be less than the average.

In this case, the average is 54 grams and 2 books are added which increases the average to 55.4, so the new books must weight more than 54 grams.

Choices A and D can be eliminated right away.

8. Probability

A bag contains 15 marbles of various colors. If 3 marbles are white, 5 are red and the rest are black, what is the probability of randomly picking out a black marble from the bag?

    a. 7/15
    b. 3/15
    c. 1/5
    d. 4/15

Solution: A

Total marbles = 15
Number of black marbles = 15 − (3 + 5) = 7
Probability of picking out a black marble = 7/15

9. Two Variables

A company paid a total of $2850 to book for 6 single rooms and 4 double rooms in a hotel for one night. Another company paid $3185 to book for 13 single rooms for one night in the same hotel. What is the cost for single and double rooms in that hotel?

    a. single= $250 and double = $345
    b. single= $254 and double = $350
    c. single = $245 and double = $305
    d. single = $245 and double = $345

Solution: D

We can determine the price of single rooms from the information given of the second company. 13 single rooms = 3185.
One single room = 3185 / 13 = 245
The first company paid for 6 single rooms at $245. 245 x 6 = $1470
Total amount paid for 4 double rooms by first company = $2850 - $1470 = $1380
Cost per double room = 1380 / 4 = $345

10. Geometry

The length of a rectangle is 5 in. more than its width. The perimeter of the rectangle is 26 in. What is the width and length of the rectangle?

    a. width = 6 inches, Length = 9 inches
    b. width = 4 inches, Length = 9 inches
    c. width =4 inches, Length = 5 inches
    d. width = 6 inches, Length = 11 inches

Solution: B

Formula for perimeter of a rectangle is 2(L + W)
p=26, so 2(L+W) = p
The length is 5 inches more than the width, so 2(w+5) + 2w = 26

2w + 10 + 2w = 26
2w + 2w = 26 - 10
4w = 16

W = 16/4 = 4 inches

L is 5 inches more than w, so L = 5 + 4 = 9 inches.

11. Totals and fractions

A basket contains 125 oranges, mangos and apples. If 3/5 of the fruits in the basket are mangos and only 2/5 of the mangos are ripe, how many ripe mangos are there in the basket?

    a. 30
    b. 68
    c. 55
    d. 47

Solution: A
Number of mangos in the basket is 3/5 x 125 = 75
Number of ripe mangos = 2/5 x 75 = 30

12. Interest

There are always four variables of any simple interest equation. With simple interest, you would be given three of these variables and be asked to solve for one unknown variable. With more complex interest problems, you would have to solve for multiple variables.

The four variables of simple interest are:

> P – Principal which refers to the original amount of money put in the account
> I – Interest or the amount of money earned as interest
> r – Rate or interest rate. This MUST ALWAYS be in decimal format and not in percentage
> t – Time or the amount of time the money is kept in

the account to earn interest

The formula for simple interest is I = P x r x t

Example 1

A customer deposits $1,000 in a savings account with a bank that offers 2% interest. How much interest will be earned after 4 years?
For this problem, we are given 3 variables as expected.

P = $1,000
t = 4 years
r = 2%
I = ?

Before we can begin solving for I using the simple interest formula, we need to first convert the rate from percentage to decimal.

2% = 2/100 = 0.02

Now we can use the formula: I = P x r x t

I = 1,000 x 0.02 x 4 = 80
This means that the $1,000 would have earned an interest of $80 after 4 years. The total amount in the account after 4 years will thus be principal + interest earned, or 1,000 + 80 = $1,080

Example 2

Sandra deposits $1400 in a savings account with a bank that offers 5% interest. How long will she have to leave the money in the bank to earn $420 as interest to buy a second hand car?

In this example, we are given:

I = $420
P = $1,400
r - 5%
t - ?

As usual, first we convert the rate from percentage to decimal 5% = 5/100 = 0.05

Next, we plug in the variables we know into the simple interest formula - I = P x r x t

420 = 1,400 x 0.05 x t
420 = 70 x t
420 = 70t
t = 420/70
t = 6

Sandra will have to leave her $1,400 in the bank for 6 years to earn her an interest of $420 at a rate of 5%.

Other important simple interest formula to remember

To use this formula below, do not convert r (rate) to decimal.

P = 100 x interest/ r x t
r = 100 x interest/p x t
t = 100 x interest/ p x r

Ratio

In mathematics, a ratio is a relationship between two numbers of the same kind[1] (e.g., objects, persons, students, spoonfuls, units of whatever identical dimension), usually expressed as "a to b" or a:b, sometimes expressed arithmetically as a dimensionless quotient of the two[2] which explicitly indicates how many times the first number contains the second (not necessarily an integer).[3] In layman's terms a ratio represents, simply, for every amount of one thing, how much there is of another thing. For example, suppose I have 10 pairs of socks for every pair of shoes then the ratio of shoes:socks would be 1:10 and the ratio of socks:shoes would be 10:1.

Notation and terminology

The ratio of numbers A and B can be expressed as:
the ratio of A to B
A is to B
A:B

A rational number which is the quotient of A divided by B
The numbers A and B are sometimes called terms with A being the antecedent and B being the consequent.

The proportion expressing the equality of the ratios A:B and C:D is written A:B=C:D or A:B::C:D. this latter form, when spoken or written in the English language, is often expressed as
A is to B as C is to D.

Again, A, B, C, D are called the terms of the proportion. A and D are called the extremes, and B and C are called the means. The equality of three or more proportions is called a continued proportion.[5]
Ratios are sometimes used with three or more terms. The dimensions of a two by four that is ten inches long are 2:4:10.

Examples

The quantities being compared in a ratio might be physical quantities such as speed or length, or numbers of objects, or amounts of particular substances. A common example of the last case is the weight ratio of water to cement in concrete, which is commonly stated as 1:4. This means that the weight of cement used is four times the weight of water used. It does not say anything about the total amounts of cement and water used, nor the amount of concrete being made. Equivalently it could be said that the ratio of cement to water is 4:1, that there is 4 times as much cement as water, or that there is a quarter (1/4) as much water as cement..
Older televisions have a 4:3 "aspect ratio," which means that the width is 4/3 of the height; modern widescreen TVs have a 16:9 aspect ratio.

Fractional

If there are 2 oranges and 3 apples, the ratio of oranges to apples is 2:3, and the ratio of oranges to the total pieces of fruit is 2:5. These ratios can also be expressed in fraction form: there are 2/3 as many oranges as apples, and 2/5 of the pieces of fruit are oranges. If orange juice concentrate is to be diluted with water in the ratio 1:4, then one part of concentrate is mixed with four parts of water, giving five parts total; the amount of orange juice concentrate is 1/4 the amount of water, while the amount of orange juice concentrate is 1/5 of the total liquid. In both ratios and fractions, it is important to be clear what is being compared to what, and beginners often make mistakes for this reason.

Number of terms

In general, when comparing the quantities of a two-quantity ratio, this can be expressed as a fraction derived from the ratio. For example, in a ratio of 2:3, the amount/size/volume/number of the first quantity will be that of the second quantity. This pattern also works with ratios with more than two terms. However, a ratio with more than two terms cannot be completely converted into a single fraction; a single fraction represents only one part of the ratio since a fraction can only compare two numbers. If the ratio deals with objects or amounts of objects, this is often expressed as "for every two parts of the first quantity there are three parts of the second quantity."

Percent and Ratio

If we multiply all quantities involved in a ratio by the same number, the ratio remains valid. For example, a ratio of 3:2 is the same as 12:8. It is usual either to reduce terms to the lowest common denominator, or to express them in parts per hundred (percent).

If a mixture contains substances A, B, C & D in the ratio 5:9:4:2 then there are 5 parts of A for every 9 parts of B, 4 parts of C and 2 parts of D. As 5+9+4+2=20, the total mixture contains 5/20 of A (5 parts out of 20), 9/20 of B, 4/20 of C, and 2/20 of D. If we divide all numbers by the total and multiply by 100, this is converted to percentages: 25% A, 45% B, 20% C, and 10% D (equivalent to writing the ratio as 25:45:20:10).

Proportion

If the two or more ratio quantities encompass all the quantities in a particular situation, for example two apples and three oranges in a fruit basket containing no other types of fruit, it could be said that "the whole" contains five parts, made up of two parts apples and three parts oranges. Here, or 40% of the whole are apples or 60% of the whole are oranges. This comparison of a specific quantity to "the whole" is sometimes called a proportion. Proportions are sometimes expressed as percentages as demonstrated above.

Perimeter, Area and Volume

Perimeter and Area (2-dimentional shapes)

Perimeter of a shape determines the length around that shape, while the area includes the space inside the shape.

Rectangle:

$P = 2a + 2b$
$A = ab$

Square

$P = 4a$
$A = a^2$

Parallelogram

$P = 2a + 2b$
$A = ah_a = bh_b$

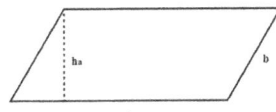

Rhombus

$P = 4a$
$A = ah = \dfrac{d_1 d_2}{2}$

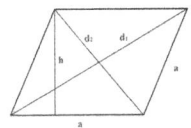

Triangle

$P = a + b + c$
$A = \dfrac{ah_a}{2} = \dfrac{bh_b}{2} = \dfrac{ch_c}{2}$

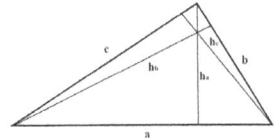

Equilateral Triangle

$P = 3a$
$A = \dfrac{a^2 \sqrt{3}}{4}$

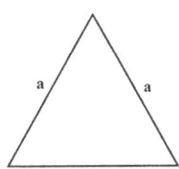

Trapezoid

$P = a + b + c + d$
$A = \dfrac{a+b}{2} h$

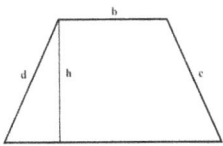

Circle

$P = 2r\pi$
$A = r^2 \pi$

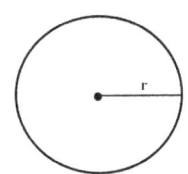

Area and Volume (3-dimentional shapes)

To calculate the area of a 3-dimentional shape, we calculate the areas of all sides and then we add them all.

To find the volume of a 3-dimentional shape, we multiply the area of the base (B) and the height (H) of the 3-dimentional shape.

$$V = BH$$

In case of a pyramid and a cone, the volume would be divided by 3.

$$V = BH/3$$

Here are some of the 3-dimentional shapes with formulas for their area and volume:

Cuboids

$A = 2(ab + bc + ac)$
$V = abc$

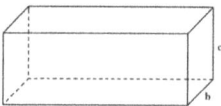

Cube

$A = 6a^2$
$V = a^3$

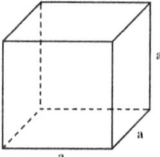

Pyramid

$A = ab + ah_a + bh_b$

$V = \dfrac{abH}{3}$

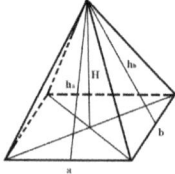

Cone

$$A = (r+s)r\pi$$

$$V = \frac{r^2 \pi H}{3}$$

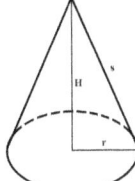

Pythagorean Geometry

If we have a right triangle ABC, where its sides (legs) are a and b and c is a hypotenuse (the side opposite the right angle), then we can establish a relationship between these sides using the following formula:

$$c^2 = a^2 + b^2$$

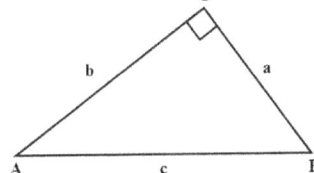

This formula is proven in the Pythagorean Theorem. There are many proofs of this theorem, but we'll look at just one geometrical proof:

If we draw squares on the right triangle's sides, then the area of the square upon the hypotenuse is equal to the sum of the areas of the squares that are upon other two sides of the triangle. Since the areas of these squares are a^2, b^2 and c^2, that is how we got the formula above.

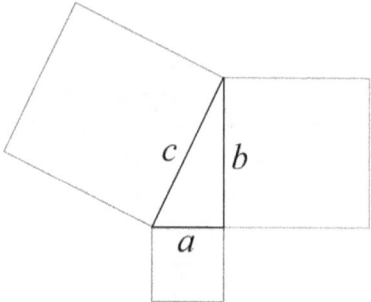

One of the famous right triangles is one with sides 3, 4 and 5. And we can see here that:

$3^2 + 4^2 = 5^2$
$9 + 16 = 25$
$25 = 25$

Example Problem:

The isosceles triangle ABC has a perimeter of 18 centimeters, and the difference between its base and legs is 3 centimeters. Find the height of this triangle.

We write the information we have about triangle ABC and we draw a picture of it for better understanding of the relation

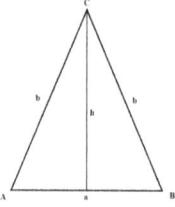

between its elements:

P=18 cm
a - b = 3 cm
h=?

We use the formula for the perimeter of the isosceles triangle, since that is what is given to us:

P = a + 2b = 18 cm

Notice that we have 2 equations with 2 variables, so we can solve it as a system of equations:

a + 2b = 18
a − b = 3 / a + 2b = 18
2a - 2b = 6 / a + 2b + 2a - 2b = 18 + 6
3a = 24
a = 24/3 = 8 cm

Now we go back to find b:
a - b = 3
8 - b = 3
b = 8 - 3
b = 5 cm

Using Pythagorean Theorem, we can find the height using a and b, because the height falls on the side a at the right angle. Notice that height cuts side a exactly in half, and that's why we use in the formula a/2. In this case, b is our hypotenuse, so we have:

$b^2 = (a/2)^2 + h^2$
$h^2 = b^2 - (a/2)^2$
$h^2 = 5^2 - (8/2)^2$
$h^2 = 5^2 - (8/2)^2$
$h^2 = 25 - 4^2$
$h^2 = 26 - 16$
$h^2 = 9$
h = 3 cm.

Language

THIS SECTION CONTAINS A SELF-ASSESSMENT AND ENGLISH TUTORIALS. The tutorials are designed to familiarize general principles and the Self-Assessment contains general questions similar to the English questions likely to be on the TABE® exam, but are not intended to be identical to the exam questions. The tutorials are not designed to be a complete English course, and it is assumed that students have some familiarity with English. If you do not understand parts of the tutorial, or find the tutorial difficult, it is recommended that you seek out additional instruction.

Tour of the TABE® Language Content

The TABE® English section has 25 questions. Below is a detailed list of the English topics likely to appear on the TABE®.

- Punctuation

- Capitalization

- Sentence structure

- Paragraph structure

- Vocabulary

- Spelling

The questions in the self-assessment are not the same as you will find on the TABE® - that would be too easy! And nobody knows what the questions will be and they change all the time. Mostly, the changes consist of substituting new questions for old, but the changes also can be new question formats or styles, changes to the number of questions in each section, changes to the time limits for each section, and combining sections. So while the format and exact wording of the questions may differ slightly, and changes from year to year, if you can answer the questions below, you will have no problem with the English section of the TABE®.

English Self-Assessment

The purpose of the self-assessment is:

- Identify your strengths and weaknesses.

- Develop your personalized study plan (above)

- Get accustomed to the TABE® format

- Extra practice – the self-assessments are almost a full 3rd practice test!

- Provide a baseline score for preparing your study schedule.

Since this is a self-assessment, and depending on how confident you are with English, timing yourself is optional. The TABE® has 25 questions, to be answered in 25 minutes. This self-assessment has 45 questions, so allow about 45 minutes to complete.

Once complete, use the table below to assess your understanding of the content, and prepare your study schedule described in chapter 1.

80% - 100%	Excellent – you have mastered the content
60 – 79%	Good. You have a working knowledge. Even though you can just pass this section, you may want to review the Tutorials and do some extra practice to see if you can improve your mark.
40% - 59%	Below Average. You do not understand the Language content. Review the tutorials, and retake this quiz again in a few days, before proceeding to the rest of the practice test questions.
Less than 40%	Poor. You have a very limited understanding of English. Please review the Tutorials, and retake this quiz again in a few days, before proceeding to the practice test questions.

English Answer Sheet

	A	B	C	D	E		A	B	C	D	E
1	○	○	○	○	○	26	○	○	○	○	○
2	○	○	○	○	○	27	○	○	○	○	○
3	○	○	○	○	○	28	○	○	○	○	○
4	○	○	○	○	○	29	○	○	○	○	○
5	○	○	○	○	○	30	○	○	○	○	○
6	○	○	○	○	○	31	○	○	○	○	○
7	○	○	○	○	○	32	○	○	○	○	○
8	○	○	○	○	○	33	○	○	○	○	○
9	○	○	○	○	○	34	○	○	○	○	○
10	○	○	○	○	○	35	○	○	○	○	○
11	○	○	○	○	○	36	○	○	○	○	○
12	○	○	○	○	○	37	○	○	○	○	○
13	○	○	○	○	○	38	○	○	○	○	○
14	○	○	○	○	○	39	○	○	○	○	○
15	○	○	○	○	○	40	○	○	○	○	○
16	○	○	○	○	○	41	○	○	○	○	○
17	○	○	○	○	○	42	○	○	○	○	○
18	○	○	○	○	○	43	○	○	○	○	○
19	○	○	○	○	○	44	○	○	○	○	○
20	○	○	○	○	○	45	○	○	○	○	○
21	○	○	○	○	○	46	○	○	○	○	○
22	○	○	○	○	○	47	○	○	○	○	○
23	○	○	○	○	○	48	○	○	○	○	○
24	○	○	○	○	○	49	○	○	○	○	○
25	○	○	○	○	○	50	○	○	○	○	○

Directions: For questions 1 - 5, choose the correct punctuation mark.

1. Sit up straight _____

    a. ;
    b. ?
    c. .
    d. :

2. They asked what time the department store would open _____

    a. ?
    b. .
    c. ,
    d. ;

3. Who do you think will win the contest _____

    a. .
    b. !
    c. ?
    d. ,

4. Four extra guests are coming to dinner _____

    a. .
    b. ?
    c. !
    d. ;

5. This is absolutely incredible ____

    a. !
    b. .
    c. :
    d. ;

6. Choose the sentence with the correct punctuation and capitalization.

    a. He looked closely at the headline Missing Boy Found Dead.
    b. The news headline read: "The King of Pop is Dead."
    c. The local paper printed a story about "his rise to power"
    d. Do you have any idea where Mr. Lucas is?

7. Choose the sentence with the correct punctuation and capitalization.

    a. My books, pens and pencils are missing from my bag.
    b. Vietnam China and the Philippines sent assistance to Malaysia.
    c. English French Spanish are the most popular world languages.
    d. I'm looking for unwanted euro pound or franc coins for my collection.

8. Choose the sentence with the correct punctuation and capitalization.

    a. Estrogen, and Progesterone are two important hormones.
    b. Reaching adolescence does'nt mean youre already an adult.
    c. The final stage of childhood, adolescence, is a challenging period.
    d. Do boys and girls experience puberty at the same time.

9. Choose the sentence with the correct punctuation and capitalization.

a. My fourteen-year-old brother wants to get his driver's license.

b. He was only ten-years old at the time of her death.

c. Weren't you only six-years-old when your parents migrated?

d. The year-1983 was the most difficult in my family.

10. Choose the sentence with the correct punctuation and capitalization.

a. The builder said that he would complete the building in one week's time.

b. The builder said "that he would complete the building" in one weeks time.

c. The builder said that he would complete the building in one weeks' time.

d. The builder said that he would complete the building in one weeks time.

11. Combine the following two sentences into one sentence with the same meaning.

They will attend the function.

They are invited.

a. Because they will be attending the function, they are invited.

b. Although they are invited, they will attend the function.

c. They are invited to the function, so they will attend.

d. As they are attending the function, they are invited.

12. Combine the following two sentences into one sentence with the same meaning.

I am not going to come.

It stops raining.

    a. After it stops raining I am not going to come.

    b. I am not going to come since it stops raining.

    c. I am not going to come so it stops raining.

    d. I am not going to come unless it stops raining.

13. Combine the following two sentences into one sentence with the same meaning.

Mary will join the group.

Mary's parents agree.

    a. Her parents agree but Mary will join the group.

    b. Only if her parents agree will Mary join the group.

    c. Mary will join the group even though her parents agree.

    d. Mary will join the group but also her parents agree.

14. Combine the following two sentences into one sentence with the same meaning.

He became ill.

He ate excessively.

    a. Even though he ate excessively, he became ill.

    b. He became ill unless he ate excessively.

    c. Except he became ill, he ate excessively.

    d. He ate excessively and he therefore became ill.

15. Combine the following two sentences into one sentence with the same meaning.

John will speak to you.

You will send John an apology.

a. Although you will send John an apology he will speak to you.

b. John will speak to you and you will send him an apology.

c. John will speak to you so that you will send him an apology.

d. You will send John an apology unless he will speak to you.

Directions: For questions 16 - 20 below, you are given a topic sentence. Choose the sentence which best develops the given topic sentence.

16. Garlic is an important ingredient in Italian dishes.

a. Italian pasta is an essential item in any cupboard.

b. Garlic belongs to the same species as onions.

c. It greatly enhances the flavor of pasta dishes.

d. Italians are some of the most welcoming people.

17. Government public transportation systems are often inefficient.

a. People prefer to travel by car because they get to their destinations faster.

b. The cost for public transportation varies from state to state.

c. Governments need to do more to promote public transport.

d. Driving by bus is not any safer than driving by car.

18. Bringing the right equipment is crucial to safety in the woods.

a. Don't panic if you become lost or get lonely in the woods.

b. More than 20,000 Black Beers live in the wild in Idaho's forest.

c. Item such as a sleeping bags and warm clothing are a top priority.

d. Camp food can taste nasty, depending on how it is prepared.

19. Every home should have a well-stocked first-aid kit.

a. Include a flashlight with extra batteries, bandages and aspirin.

b. Hydrogen peroxide is a compound used in cleansing wounds.

c. Johnson and Johnson made the first first-aid kit in the 1800s.

d. A fire extinguisher is a device used to put out small fires.

20. Men and women in love are often blind to each other's faults.

a. Age does not determine the success of a relationship.

b. Compatibility and financial security are often ignored.

c. Hundreds of dating sites have popped up over the internet.

d. Parents disagree on the age at which teenagers should date.

Questions 21 - 25 refer to the following passage.

Read the passage below and look at the numbered, underlined phrases. Choose the answer that is written correctly for each underlined part.

The sun, the enormous ball consisting of hot plasma, stands as the center of the solar system to which earth belong (21), the Milky Way. Essential it is, to life on this planet, as it is the primary source of energy. The sun determines climate, weather and supports all life on our planet. There's no solar system without the sun and, of course, no Earth without the solar system.

However, not all that glitters is gold, as most of us would know (22). These same rays of sunshine, with their life-giving power, are also lethally dangerous. The sun attacks the earth with ultraviolet (UV) radiation. Scientists has long discovered (23) that the sun, this weapon of mass destruction, is actually a wolf dressed in sheep's clothing.

These same scientists tell us that the earth once had the power to fight off the hazardous ultraviolet rays that the sun hurls at it on a daily basis. Now, because no fault on his own (24), the sun has become our worst feared monster. The ozone layer, that precious shield that protects us from those fatal rays, is being eaten away, day after day, by no one but us.

The man-made chemicals that we allow to seep into the atmosphere have turned on us and are helping the sun wreak havoc on the planet. Most sensible people know (25) UV radiation can harm the skin. But there's much more. Even our eyes, the windows to our souls, are in jeopardy. The long-term effects of the sun's destructive onslaught cannot be avoided. In fact, the effects are being felt now. Weather changes, global warming and skin cancers are only a few of the evidences that the sun is no longer our friend.

21. Choose the correct version.

    a. to which earth belongs

    b. to that earth belongs

    c. of which earth belong

    d. Correct as is.

22. Choose the correct version.

    a. had known

    b. would have known

    c. have come to know

    d. Correct as is.

23. Choose the correct version.

    a. have long discovers

    b. have long discovered

    c. will have long discovered

    d. Correct as is.

24. Choose the correct version.

    a. by no fault on his own

    b. with no fault of its own

    c. through no fault of its own

    d. Correct as is.

25. Choose the correct version.

    a. Most sensible peoples know

    b. Most sensible people knows

    c. Greater sensible people know

    d. Correct as is.

For questions 26 - 30, choose the word that best completes both sentences.

26. His art is very _____.

That sidewalk is only meant for _____.

    a. pedestrian
    b. avant–garde
    c. extreme
    d. none of the above

27. Gasoline is very _____.

She has a very _____ temper.

    a. volatile
    b. flammable
    c. inert
    d. none of the above

28. The tree has _____ over millions of years.

He was _____ at the horror movie.

    a. scared
    b. petrified
    c. rotted
    d. none of the above

29. He loves crowded places and has always been very _____.

She is not very social or _____.

    a. thoughtful
    b. introverted
    c. gregarious
    d. none of the above

30. I always _____ with my brother.

They always get along and never _____ .

    a. bicker
    b. socialize
    c. debate
    d. none of the above

For questions 31 - 35, choose the word that best completes the sentence.

31. When Joe broke his _____ in a skiing accident, his entire leg was in a cast.

    a. Ankle
    b. Humerus
    c. Wrist
    d. Femur

32. Alan had to learn the _____ system of numbering when his family moved to Great Britain.

    a. American
    b. Decimal
    c. Metric
    d. Fingers and toes

33. After Lisa's aunt had her tenth child, Lisa found that she had more than twenty _____ .

    a. Uncles
    b. Friends
    c. Stepsisters
    d. Cousins

34. George is very serious about _____, and recently joined the American Scholastic Association.

    a. Schoolwork
    b. Cooking
    c. Travelling
    d. Athletics

35. She was a rabid Red Sox fan, attending every game, and demonstrating her _____ by cheering more loudly than anyone else.

    a. Knowledge
    b. Boredom
    c. Commitment
    d. Enthusiasm

Spelling

36. I don't want to get into an _____.

    a. Arguemint
    b. Arguement
    c. Argument
    d. Arguemant

37. It is not a common _____.

    a. Occurrance
    b. Ocurrence
    c. Occurrence
    d. Occurence

38. He sounded very _____.

    a. Desperate
    b. Desparate
    c. Desperete
    d. Despirate

39. I will be there _____ night.

    a. Wedesday
    b. Wendesday
    c. Wenesday
    d. Wednesday

40. I always have _____ on my fries.

    a. Kechup
    b. Ketsup
    c. Kechup
    d. Ketchup

41. Choose the phrase that is not spelled correctly.

a. Sergent at arms
b. Immediately after
c. Vacuum cleaner
d. Cross the threshold

42. Choose the phrase that is not spelled correctly.

a. Thorough investigation
b. Rythym and blues
c. Fictitious name
d. Particular concern

43. Choose the phrase that is not spelled correctly.

a. Mysterious disappearance
b. Scientific experiment
c. Miscellaneous items
d. Secret corespondence

44. Choose the phrase that is not spelled correctly.

a. Environimental disaster
b. Government action
c. Pride and prejudice
d. Severely punished

45. Choose the phrase that is not spelled correctly.

a. Permissible excuse
b. Easily defeated
c. Amateur wrestling
d. Impliment the changes

Answer Key

1. C
A period or an exclamation mark is used to end an imperative sentence, that is, at the end of a direction or a command.

2. B
A period is used to end an indirect question. An indirect question is always a part of a declarative sentence and it does not require an answer.

3. C
A question mark is used to end an interrogative sentence, that is, at the end of a direct question which requires an answer.

4. B
Use a question mark to end a statement that is intended as a question.

5. A
Use an exclamation mark to end an exclamatory sentence, that is, at the end of a statement showing strong emotion.

6. B
Choice D is incorrect as "Mr." should be capitalized.
Choice A is incorrect, as the headline should be in quotation marks.
Choice C is incorrect as the title of the story should be in sentence case.

7. A
Commas are missing in all other choices.

8. C
Choice A has a comma after estrogen and before "and."
Choice B is missing an apostrophe in "you're."
Choice D is missing a question mark.

9. A
Choices B, C and D have hyphens where they are not needed.

10. A
Choices C and D have incorrect use of apostrophes. Choice B has no apostrophe and incorrect use of quotation marks.

11. C
12. D
13. B
14. D
15. B
16. B
17. C
18. C
19. C
20. B
21. A
22. C
23. B
24. C
25. D

26. A
Pedestrian: (1) Ordinary, dull; everyday; unexceptional. (2) a person walking along a road or in a developed area.

27. A
Volatile: Explosive.

28. B
Petrified: (1) To harden organic matter by permeating with water and depositing dissolved minerals. (2) so frightened that one is unable to move; terrified.

29. C
Gregarious: A
Describing one who enjoys being in crowds and socializing.

30. A
Bicker: To quarrel in a tiresome, insulting manner.

31. D
Femur: the bone of the thigh or upper hind limb, articulating at the hip and the knee.

32. C
Metric: a system or standard of measurement.

33. D
Cousins

34. A
Schoolwork

35. D
Enthusiasm: intense and eager enjoyment, interest, or approval.

Spelling

36. C
Argument is the correct spelling.

37. C
Occurrence is the correct spelling.

38. A
Desperate is the correct spelling.

39. D
Wednesday is the correct spelling.

40. D
Ketchup is the correct spelling.

41. A
Sergent at arms is incorrect. The correct spelling is sergeant at arms.

42. B
Rythym and blues is incorrect. The correct spelling is rhythm and blues.

43. D
Corespondence is incorrect. The correct spelling is correspondence.

44. A

Environimental is incorrect. The correct spelling is environmental.

45. D

Impliment is incorrect. The correct spelling is implement.

English Grammar and Punctuation Tutorials

Capitalization

Although many of the rules for capitalization are pretty straight forward, there are several tricky points that are important to review.

Starting a Sentence

Everyone knows that you need to capitalize the first letter of the first word in a sentence, but is it really all that easy to figure out where one sentence starts and another stops? Take these three examples:

That was the moment it really sunk in: There would be no hockey this year.

It was April and that could mean only one thing: baseball.

We played for hours before heading home; everyone felt tired and happy.

In the first example, the first letter after the colon is capitalized while in the second example it is not. That is because everything after the first example's colon is a complete sentence, while after example two's colon there is only one word. In example three you have what could be a complete sentence ("everyone felt tired and happy"), but which is not because it follows a semicolon, making it just another clause instead.

Within a sentence you can have an additional complete sentence if the sentence follows a colon. However, if what could be a complete sentence follows a semicolon, it is a clause and does not get capitalized.

Remember that the same rules apply for quotation marks

that apply for colons: A complete sentence inside quotation marks is capitalized, but a single word or phrase is not.

Proper Nouns

The first letter of all proper nouns needs to be capitalized. There are many categories of proper noun. The most common proper nouns are the specific names of people (such as Bill), places (such as Germany) or things (such as Honda Civic). However, there are several less obvious categories of words that should be capitalized as proper nouns.

Historical events such as World War II or the California Gold Rush need to be capitalized.

The names of celestial bodies such as Orion's Belt need to be capitalized.

The names of ethnicities such as African-American or Hispanic need to be capitalized.

Relationship words that replace a person's name such as Mom, Doctor and Mister need to be capitalized. However, this only happens when you use the word to replace the person's name. In the sentence, "My mom went to the store," you do not capitalize it, while in the sentence, "Hey Mom, did you get toothpaste at the store?" you do capitalize it.

Geographical locations are capitalized. This can be tricky because capitalized geographical locations and non-capitalized directions are easy to confuse. Saying, "We drove south for hours," is a direction, so the word "south" should not be capitalized. However, when saying, "While in the United States, we drove to the South to look at Civil War battle fields," you do capitalize the word "South." The difference is that in the first sentence "south" is just the direction you drove. In the second sentence "the South" is a specific region of the United States that formed itself into the Confederacy during the US Civil War.

Proper Adjectives

Proper adjectives are the adjective forms of proper nouns. People from Germany are German; people from Canada are Canadian. German and Canadian are proper adjectives because they are forms of proper nouns that are used to describe other nouns.

Titles of Works

Titles of works are generally capitalized following a specific pattern. Capitalize all the important words in a sentence. Do not capitalize unimportant words such as prepositions and articles.

For example: Alien Spaceship Spotted over Many of the World's Capitals

Notice that the prepositions "over" and "of," and the article "the" are the only non-capitalized words in the sentence.

Colons and Semicolons

Within a sentence there are several different types of punctuation marks that can denote a pause. Each of these punctuation marks has different rules when it comes to its structure and usage, so we will look at each one in turn.

Colons

The colon is used primarily to introduce information. It can start lists such as in the sentence, "There were several things Susan had to get at the store: bread, cereal, lettuce and tomatoes." Or a colon points out specific information, such as in the sentence, "It was only then that the group fully realized what had happened: The Martian invasion had begun."

Note that if the information after the colon is a complete sentence, you capitalize and punctuate it exactly like you would a sentence. If, however, it does not constitute a complete sentence, you don't have to capitalize anything. ("Peering out the window Meredith saw them: zombies.")

Semicolons

Semicolons are super commas. They denote a stronger stop than a comma does, but they are still weaker than a period, not quite capable of ending a sentence. Semicolons are primarily used to separate independent clauses that are not being separated by a coordinating conjunction. ("Chris went to the store; he bought chips and salsa.") Semicolons can only do this, however, when the ideas in each clause are related. For instance, the sentence, "It's raining outside; my sister went to the movies," is not a proper usage of the semicolon since those clauses have nothing to do with each other.

Semicolons can also be used in lists if one or more element in the list is itself made up of a smaller list. If you want to write a list of things you plan to bring to a picnic, and those things only include a Frisbee, a chair and some pasta salad, you would not need to use a semicolon. But if you also wanted to bring plastic knives, forks and spoons, you would need to write your sentence like this: "For our picnic I am bringing a Frisbee; a chair; plastic knives, forks and spoons; and some pasta salad."

Using semicolons like this preserves the smaller list that you have in your larger list.

Commas

Commas are probably the most commonly used punctuation mark in English. Commas can break the flow of writing to give it a more natural sounding style, and they are the main punctuation mark used to separate ideas. Commas also separate lists, introductory adverbs, introductory prepositional phrases, dates and addresses.

The most rigid way that commas are used is when separating clauses. There are two primary types of clauses in a sentence, independent and subordinate (sometimes called dependent). Independent clauses are clauses that express a complete thought, such as, "Tim went to the store." Subordinate clauses, on the other hand, only express partial thoughts that serve to expand on an independent clause, such as, "after the game ended," which you can see is clearly not a complete sentence. (You will learn more about clauses in different lessons.)

The rule for commas with clauses is that a comma must separate the clauses when a subordinate clause comes first in a sentence: "After the game ended, Tim went to the store." But there should not be a comma when a subordinate clause follows an independent clause: "Tim went to the store after the game ended." If you leave the comma out of the first example, you have a run-on sentence. If you add one into the second example, you have a comma-splice error. Also, when you have two independent clauses joined with a coordinating conjunction, you need to separate them with a comma. "Tim went to the store, and Beth went home."

Commas are also used to separate items in a list. This area of English is unfortunately less clear than it should be, with two separate rules depending on what standard you are following. To understand the two different rules, let's pretend you are having a party at your house, and you are making a list of refreshments your friends will want. You may decide to serve three things: 1) pizza 2) chips 3) drinks. There are two different rules governing how you should punctuate this. According to many grammar books, you would write this as, "At the store I will buy pizza, chips, and drinks." This variation puts a comma after each item in the list. It is the version that the style books used in most college English and history courses will prefer, so it is probably the one you should follow. However, the Associated Press style guide, which is used in college journalism classes and at newspapers and magazines, says the sentence should be written like this: "At the store I will buy pizza, chips and drinks." Here you only use a comma between the first two words, letting the word "and" act as the separator between the last two.

Another important place to use commas is when you have a modifier that describes an element of a sentence, but that does not directly follow the thing it describes. Look at the sentence: "Tim went over to visit Beth, watching the full moon along the way." In this sentence there is no confusion about who is "watching the full moon"; it is Tim, probably as he walks to Beth's house. If you remove the comma, however, you get this: "Tim went over to visit Beth watching the full moon along the way." Now it sounds as though Beth is watching the full moon, and we are forced to wonder what "way" the moon is traveling along.

Commas are also used when adding introductory prepositional phrases and introductory adverbs to sentences. A comma is always needed following an introductory adverb. ("Quickly, Jody ran to the car.") Commas are even necessary when you have an adverb introducing a clause within a sentence, even if the clause not the first clause of the sentence. ("Amanda wanted to go to the movie; however, she knew her homework was more important.")

With introductory prepositional phrases you only add a comma if the phrase (or if a group of introductory phrases) is five or more words long. Thus, the sentence you just read did not have a comma following its introductory prepositional phrase ("With introductory prepositional phrases") because it was only four words. Compare that to this sentence with a five word introductory phrase: "After the ridiculously long class, the friends needed to relax."

The last main way that commas are used in sentences is to separate out information that does not need to be there. For instance, "My cousin Hector, who wore a blue hat at the party, thought you were funny." The fact that Hector wore a blue hat is interesting, but it is not vital to the sentence; it could be removed and not changed the sentence's meaning. Therefore, it gets commas around it. Along these lines you should remember that any clause introduced by the word that is considered to provide essential information to the sentence and should not get commas around it. Conversely, any clause starting with the word which is considered nonessential and should not get commas around it.

How to Answer English Grammar Multiple Choice - Verb Tense

This tutorial is designed to help you answer English Grammar multiple choice questions as well as a very quick refresher on verb tenses. It is assumed that you have some familiarity with the verb tenses covered here. If you find these questions difficulty or do not understand the tense construction, we recommend you seek out additional instruction.

Tenses Covered

1. Past Progressive
2. Present Perfect
3. Present Perfect Progressive
4. Present Progressive
5. Simple Future
6. Simple Future – "Going to" Form
7. Past Perfect Progressive
8. Future Perfect Progressive
9. Future Perfect
10. Future Progressive
11. Past Perfect

1. The Past Progressive Tense

How to Recognize This Tense

He *was running* very fast when he fell.

They *were drinking* coffee when he arrived.

About the Past Progressive Tense

This tense is used to speak of an action that was in progress in the past when another event occurred.

The action was unfolding at a point in the past.

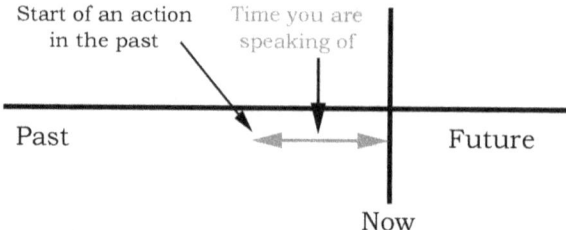

Past Progressive Tense Construction

This tense is formed by using the past tense of the verb "to be" plus the present participle of the main verb.

Sample Question

Bill _____ lunch when we arrived.

    a. will eat
    b. is eating
    c. eats
    d. was eating

How to Answer This Type of Question

1. First examine the question for clues about the time frame.

The sentence ends with "when we arrived," so we know the time frame is a point ("when") in the past (arrived).

The correct answer will refer to an ongoing action at a point of time in the past.

2. Examine the choices and eliminate any obviously incorrect answers.

Choice A is the future tense so we can eliminate.

Choice B is the present continuous so we can eliminate.

Choice C is present tense so we can eliminate.

Choice D refers to an action that takes place at a point of time in the past ("was eating").

2. The Present Perfect Tense

How to Recognize This Tense

I *have had* enough to eat.

We *have been* to Paris many times.

I *have known* him for five years.

I *have been* coming here since I was a child.

About the Present Perfect Tense

This tense expresses the idea that something happened (or didn't happen) at an unspecific time in the past up until the present. The action happened at an unspecified time in the past. (If there is a specific time mentioned, the simple past tense is used.) It can be used for repeated action, accomplishments, changes over time and uncompleted action.

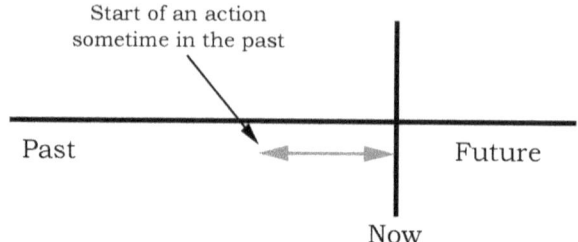

Present Perfect Tense Construction

It is also used with "for" and "since."

This tense is formed by using the present tense of the verb "to have" plus the past participle of the main verb.

Sample Question

I _____ these birds many times.

    a. am seeing
    b. will saw
    c. have seen
    d. have saw

How to Answer This Type of Question

1. First examine the question for clues about the time frame.

"Many times" tells us that the action is repeated and in the past.

2. Examine the choices and eliminate any obviously incorrect answers.

Choice A, "am seeing" is incorrect because it is a continuing action, i.e. in the present; it also doesn't use a form of 'have'.

Choice B is grammatically incorrect.

Choice C is tells of something that has happened in the past and is now over. Best choice so far.

Choice D is grammatically incorrect.

3. The Present Perfect Progressive Tense

How to Recognize This Tense

We *have been seeing* a lot of rainy days.

I *have been reading* some very good books.

About the Present Perfect Progressive Tense

This tense expresses the idea that something happened (or didn't happen) in the relatively recent past, but <u>the action is not finished.</u> It is used to express the duration of the action.

NOTE: The present perfect speaks of an action that happened sometime in the past, but this action is finished. In the present perfect progressive tense, the action that started in the past is still going on.

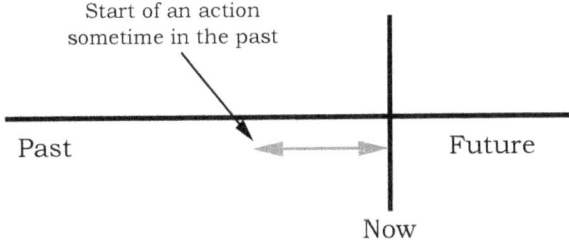

Present Perfect Progressive Tense Construction

This tense is formed by using the present tense of the verb "to have," plus "been," plus the present participle of the main verb.

Sample Question

Bill _____ there for two hours.

    a. sits

b. sitting

c. has been sitting

d. will sat

How to Answer This Type of Question

1. First examine the question for clues about the time frame.

"For two hours" tells us that the action, "sits," is continuous up to now, and may continue into the future.

Note this sentence could also be the simple past tense,

Bill sat there for two hours.

Or the future tense,

Bill will sit there for two hours.

However, these are not among the choices.

2. Examine the choices and eliminate any obviously incorrect answers.

Choice A is incorrect because it is the present tense.
Choice B is incorrect because it is the present continuous.
Choice C is correct. "Has been sitting" expresses a continuous action in the past that isn't finished.
Choice D is grammatically incorrect.

4. The Present Progressive Tense

How to Recognize This Tense

We *are having* a delicious lunch.

They *are driving* much too fast.

About the Present Progressive Tense

This tense is used to express what the action is <u>right now</u>.

The action started in the recent past, and is continuing into the future.

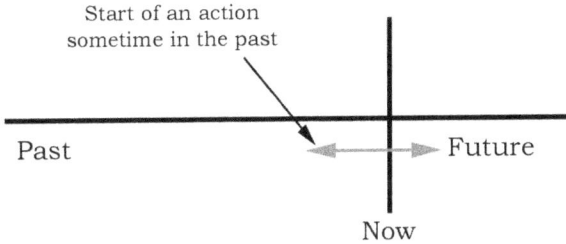

Present Perfect Tense Construction

The Present Progressive Tense is formed by using the present tense of "to be" plus the present participle of the main verb.

Sample Question

She _____ very hard these days.

    a. works

    b. is working

    c. will work

    d. worked

How to Answer This Type of Question

1. First examine the question for clues about the time frame.

The end of the sentence includes "these days" which tell us the action started in the past, continues into the present, and may continue into the future.

2. Examine the choices and eliminate any obviously incorrect answers.

Choice A, the simple present is incorrect.
Choice B, "is working" is correct.
Check the other two choices just to be sure. Choice C is

future tense, and Choice D is past tense, so they can be eliminated.

The correct answer is Choice B.

5. The Simple Future Tense

How to Recognize This Tense

I *will see* you tomorrow.
We *will drive* the car.

About the Simple Future Tense

This tense shows that the action will happen some time in the future.

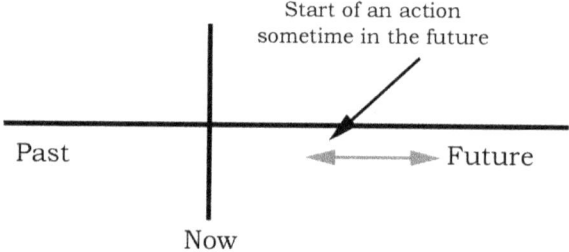

Simple Future Tense Construction

The tense is formed by using "will" plus the root form of the verb. (The root form of the verb is the infinitive without "to." Examples: read, swim.)

Sample Question

We _____ to Paris next year.

    a. went

    b. had been

    c. will go

d. go

How to Answer This Type of Question

1. First examine the question for clues about the time frame.

The last two words of the sentence, "next year," clearly identify this sentence as referring to the future.

2. Examine the choices and eliminate any obviously incorrect answers.

Choice A is the past tense and can be eliminated.

Choice B is the past perfect tense and can be eliminated.

Choice D is the simple present and can be eliminated.

Choice C is the only one left and is the correct simple future tense.

6. The Simple Future Tense – The "Going to" Form

How to Recognize This Tense

I *am going to* see you tomorrow.

We *are going to* drive the car.

About the Simple Future Tense

This form of the future tense is used to show the intention of doing something in the future. (This is the strict grammatical meaning, but in daily speech, it is often used interchangeably with the simple future tense, the "will" form.)

The tense is formed by using the present conditional tense of "to go," plus the infinitive of the verb.

Sample Question

I _____ shopping in an hour.

   a. go
   b. have gone
   c. am going to go
   d. went

How to Answer This Type of Question

1. First examine the question for clues about the time frame.

"In an hour" clearly identifies the action as taking place in the future.

2. Examine the choices and eliminate any obviously incorrect answers.

Choice A is the simple present tense and can be eliminated.

Choice B is the past perfect and can be eliminated.

Choice C is the correct answer.

Choice D is the past tense and can be eliminated.

7. The Past Perfect Progressive Tense

How to Recognize This Tense

I *had been sleeping* for an hour when you phoned.

We *had been eating* our dinner when they all came into the dining room.

About the Past Perfect Progressive Tense

This tense is used to show that the action had been going on for a period of time in the past when another action, also in the past, occurred.

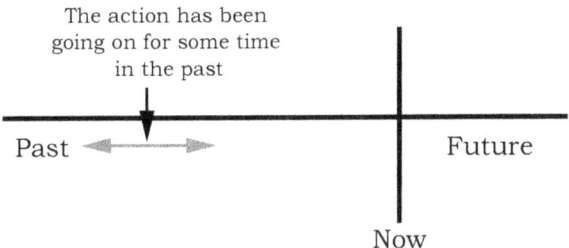

Past Perfect Tense Construction

The tense is formed by using the past perfect tense of the verb "to be" plus the present participle of the main verb.

Sample Question

How long _____ you _____ when I saw you?

    a. are _____ running

    b. had _____ running

    c. had _____ been running

    d. was _____ running

How to Answer This Type of Question

1. First examine the question for clues about the time frame.

"When I saw" tells us the sentence happened at a point of time ("when") in the past ("saw").

2. Examine the choices and eliminate any obviously incorrect answers.

Choice A, "are running" is incorrect and can be eliminated.

Choice B, "Had ___ running" is grammatically incorrect and can be eliminated.

Choice C is correct.

Choice D is grammatically incorrect so the answer is Choice C.

8. Future Perfect Progressive Tense

How to Recognize This Tense

I *will have been working* here for two years in March.

I *will have been driving* for four hours when I get there, so I will be tired.

About the Future Perfect Progressive Tense

This tense is used to show that the action continues up to a point of time in the future.

Future Prefect Progressive Tense Construction

This tense is formed by using the future perfect tense of "to be" plus the present participle of the main verb.

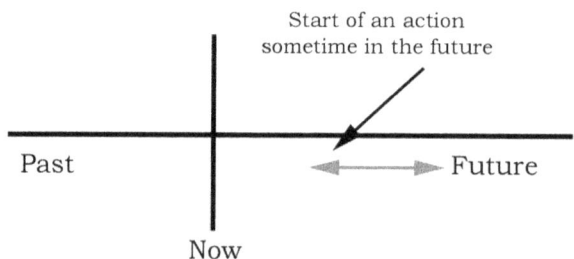

Sample Question

_____ you _____ all the time I am gone?

    a. have ____ been working
    b. will ____ have been working
    c. are ____ worked
    d. will ____ worked

How to Answer This Type of Question

1. First examine the question for clues about the time frame.

"All the time I am gone" refers to an action in the future ("time I am gone") and the action is progressive ("all the time"). The progressive action means the correct choice will be a verb tense that ends in "ing."

2. Examine the choices and eliminate any obviously incorrect answers.

Choice A, the past perfect, refers to a past continuous event and is also grammatically incorrect in the sentence, so Choice A can be eliminated.

Choice B looks correct because it refers to an action will be going on for a period of time in the future.

Examine Choices C and D just to be sure. Both choices are grammatically incorrect and can be eliminated.
Choice B is the correct answer.

9. The Future Perfect Tense

How to Recognize This Tense

By next November, I *will have received* my promotion.

By the time he gets home, she is going *to have cleaned* the entire house.

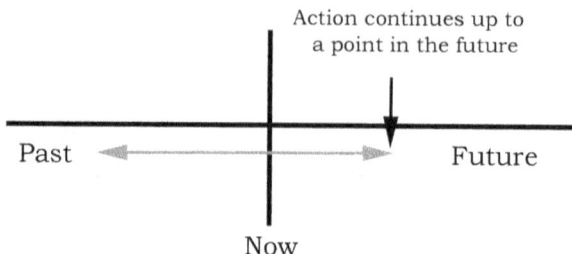

About the Future Perfect Tense

The future perfect tense expresses action in the future before another action in the future. This is the past in the future.

For example:

He *will have prepared* dinner when she arrives.

Future Perfect Tense Construction

This tense is formed by "will + have + past participle."

Sample Question

They _____ their seats before the game begins.

    a. will have find

    b. will find

    c. will have found

    d. found

How to Answer This Type of Question

1. First examine the question for clues about the time frame.

This question could be several different tenses. The only clue about the time frame is "before the game begins," which refers to a specific point of time.

We know it isn't in the past, because "begins" is incorrect for the past tense. So the question is about something that happens in the future, before another event in the future.

2. Examine the choices and eliminate any obviously incorrect answers.

Choice A can be eliminated as incorrect.
Choice B looks good, so mark it and check the others before making a final decision.
Choice C is the past perfect and can be eliminated because the time frame is incorrect.
Choice D is the simple past tense and can be eliminated for the same reason.

10. Future Progressive Tense

How to Recognize This Tense

The teams *will be playing* soccer when we arrive.

At 3:45 the soccer fans *will be waiting* for the game to start at 4:00 o'clock

At 3:45 the soccer players *will be preparing* to play at 4:00 o'clock

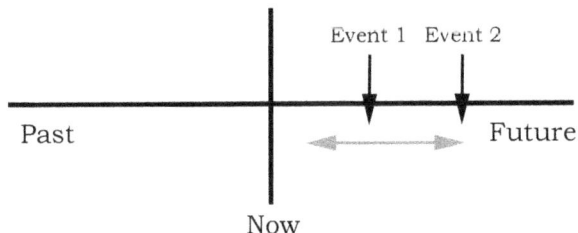

About the Future Progressive Tense

The future progressive tense talks about a continuing action in the future.

Future Progressive Tense Construction

will+ be + (root form) + ing = will be playing

Sample Question

Many excited fans _____ a bus to see the game at 4:00.

    a. catch

    b. catching

    c. have been catching

    d. will be catching

How to Answer This Type of Question

1. First examine the question for clues about the time frame.

"At 4:00," tells us the sentence is either in the past OR in the future.

2. Examine the choices and eliminate any obviously incorrect answers.

From the time frame of the sentence, the answer will be past or future tense.

Choice A is the present tense and can be eliminated.
Choice B is the present continuous tense and can be eliminated.
Choice C is the past perfect continuous and can be eliminated.
Choice D is the only one left. Quickly examining the tense, it is future progressive and is correct in the sentence.

11. The Past Perfect Tense

How to Recognize This Tense

The party *had* just *started* when the coach arrived.

We *had waited* for twenty minutes when the bus finally came.

About the Past Perfect

The past perfect tense talks about two events that happened in the past and establishes which event happened first.

Another example is, "We had eaten when he arrived."

The two events are "eat" and "he arrived." From the sentence above the past perfect tense tells us the first event, "eat" happened before the second event, "he arrived."

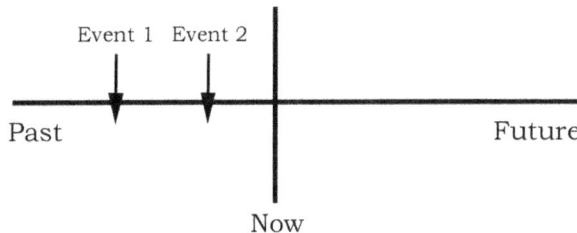

I had already eaten when my friends arrived.

Past Perfect Tense Construction

The past perfect is formed by "have" plus the past participle.

Sample Question

It was time to go home after they _____ the game.

    a. will win

    b. win

    c. had won

d. wins

How to Answer This Type of Question

1. First examine the question for clues about the time frame.

"Was" tells us the sentence happened in the past. Also notice there are two events, "go home" and "after the game."

2. Examine the choices and eliminate any obviously incorrect answers.

Choice A is the future tense and can be eliminated. Choice B is the simple present and can be eliminated. Choice C is the past perfect and orders the two events in the past. Choice D is the present tense and incorrect and can be eliminated, so Choice C is the correct answer.

Common English Usage Mistakes - A Quick Review

Like some parts of English grammar, usage is definitely going to be on the exam and there isn't any tricky strategies or shortcuts to help you get through this section.
Here is a quick review of common usage mistakes.

1. May and Might

'May' can act as a principal verb, which can express permission or possibility.

Examples:

Lets wait, the meeting may have started.
May I begin now?

'May' can act as an auxiliary verb, which an expresses a purpose or wish

Examples:

May you find favour in the sight of your employer.

May your wishes come true.
People go to school so that they may be educated.

The past tense of may is might.

Examples:

I asked if I might begin

'Might' can be used to signify a weak or slim possibility or polite suggestion.

Examples:

You might find him in his office, but I doubt it.
You might offer to help if you want to.

2. Lie and Lay

The verb lay should always take an object. The three forms of the verb lay are: laid, lay and laid.

The verb lie (recline) should not take any object. The three forms of the verb lie are: lay, lie and lain.

Examples:

Lay on the bed.
The tables were laid by the students.
Let the little kid lie.
The patient lay on the table.

The dog has lain there for 30 minutes.

Note: The verb lie can also mean "to tell a falsehood." This verb can appear in three forms: lied, lie, and lied. This is different from the verb lie (recline) mentioned above.

Examples:

The accused is fond of telling lies.
Did she lie?

3. Would and should

The past tense of shall is 'should', and so "should" generally follows the same principles as "shall."

The past tense of will is "would," and so "would" generally follows the same principles as "will."

The two verbs 'would and should' can be correctly used interchangeably to signify obligation. The two verbs also have some unique uses too. Should is used in three persons to signify obligation.

Examples:

I should go after work.
People should exercise everyday.
You should be generous.

"Would" is specially used in any of the three persons, to signify willingness, determination and habitual action.
Examples:

They would go for a test run every Saturday.
They would not ignore their duties.
She would try to be punctual.

4. Principle and Auxiliary Verbs

Two principal verbs can be used along with one auxiliary verb as long as the auxiliary verb form suits the two principal verbs.

Examples:

Several people have been employed and some promoted.

A new tree has been planted and the old has been cut down.
Again note the difference in the verb form.

5. Can and Could

A. Can is used to express capacity or ability.

Examples:

I can complete the assignment today
He can meet his target.
B. Can is also used to express permission.

Examples:

Yes, you can begin

In the sentence below, "can" was used to mean the same thing as "may." However, the difference is that the word "can" is used for negative or interrogative sentences, while "may" is used in affirmative sentences to express possibility.

Examples:

They may be correct.   Positive sentence - use may.
Can this statement be correct? A question using "can."
It cannot be correct. Negative sentence using "can."

The past tense of can is could. It can serve as a principal verb when it is used to express its own meaning.

Examples:

Despite the difficulty of the test, he could still perform well. "Could" here is used to express ability.

6. Ought

The verb ought should normally be followed by the word to.

Examples:

I *ought to* close shop now.

The verb 'ought' expresses:
A. Desirability

You ought to wash your hands before eating.   It is desirable to wash your hands.

B. Probability

She ought to be on her way back by now.   She is probably on her way.

C. Moral obligation or duty

The government ought to protect the oppressed.   It is the government's duty to protect the oppressed.

7. Raise and Rise

Rise
The verb rise means to go up, or to ascend.
The verb rise can appear in three forms, rose, rise, and risen. The verb should not take an object.

Examples:

The bird rose very slowly.
The trees rise above the house.
My aunt has risen in her career.
Raise
The verb raise means to increase, to lift up.
The verb raise can appear in three forms, raised, raise and raised.

Examples:

He raised his hand.
The workers requested a raise.
Do not raise that subject.

8. Past Tense and Past Participle

Pay attention to the proper use of these verbs: sing, show, ring, awake, fly, flow, begin, hang and sink.

Mistakes usually occur when using the past participle and past tense of these verbs as they are often mixed up.

Each of these verbs can appear in three forms:

Sing, Sang, Sung.
Show, Showed, Showed/Shown.
Ring, Rang, Rung.
Awake, awoke, awaken
Fly, Flew, Flown.
Flow, Flowed, Flowed.
Begin, Began, Begun.
Hang, Hanged, Hanged (a criminal)
Hang, Hung, Hung (a picture)
Sink, Sank, Sunk.

Examples:

The stranger rang the door bell. (simple past tense)
I have rung the door bell already. (past participle - an action

completed in the past)

The stone sank in the river. (simple past tense)
The stone had already sunk. (past participle - an action completed in the past)
The meeting began at 4:00.
The meeting has begun.

9. Shall and Will

When speaking informally, the two can be used interchangeably. In formal writing, they must be used correctly.

"Will" is used in the second or third person, while "shall" is used in the first person. Both verbs are used to express a time or even in the future.

Examples:

I shall, We shall (First Person)
You will (Second Person)
They will (Third Person)

This principle however reverses when the verbs are to be used to express threats, determination, command, willingness, promise or compulsion. In these instances, will is now used in first person and shall in the second and third person.

Examples:

I will be there next week, no matter what.
This is a promise, so the first person "I" takes "will."

You shall ensure that the work is completed.
This is a command, so the second person "you" takes "shall."

I will try to make payments as promised.
This is a promise, so the first person "I" takes "will."

They shall have arrived by the end of the day.
This is a determination, so the third person "they" takes shall.

Note
A. The two verbs, shall and will should not occur twice in the same sentence when the same future is being referred to

Example:

I shall arrive early if my driver is here on time.

B. Will should not be used in the first person when questions are being asked

Examples:

Shall I go ?
Shall we go?

Subject Verb Agreement

Verbs in any sentence must agree with the subject of the sentence in person and number. Problems usually occur when the verb doesn't correspond with the right subject or the verb fails to match the noun close to it.

Unfortunately, there is no easy way around these principals - no tricky strategy or easy rule. You just have to memorize them.

Here is a quick review:

The verb to be, present (past)

Person	Singular	Plural
First	I am (was)	we are (were)
Second	you are (were)	you are (were)
Third	he, she, it is (was)	they are (were)

The verb to have, present (past)

Person	Singular	Plural
First	I have (had)	we have (had)
Second	you have (had)	you have (had)
Third	he, she, it has (had)	they have (had)

Regular verbs, e.g. to walk, present (past)

Person	Singular	Plural
First	I walk (walked)	we walk (walked)
Second	you walk (walked)	you walk (walked)
Third	he, she, it walks (walked)	they work (walked)

1. Every and Each

When nouns are qualified by "every" or "each," they take a singular verb even if they are joined by 'and'

Examples:

Each mother and daughter *was* a given separate test.
Every teacher and student *was* properly welcomed.

2. Plural Nouns

Nouns like measles, tongs, trousers, riches, scissors etc. are all plural.

Examples:

The trousers *are* dirty.
My scissors *have* gone missing.
The tongs *are* on the table.

3. With and As Well

Two subjects linked by "with" or "as well" should have a verb that matches the first subject.

Examples:

The pencil, with the papers and equipment, *is* on the desk.
David as well as Louis is coming.

4. Plural Nouns

The following nouns take a singular verb:

> politics, mathematics, innings, news, advice, summons, furniture, information, poetry, machinery, vacation, scenery

Examples:

The machinery *is* difficult to assemble
The furniture *has* been delivered
The scenery *was* beautiful

5. Single Entities

A proper noun in plural form that refers to a single entity requires a singular verb. This is a complicated way of saying; some things appear to be plural, but are really singular, or some nouns refer to a collection of things but the collection is really singular.

Examples:

The United Nations Organization *is* the decision maker in the matter.

Here the "United Nations Organization" is really only one "thing" or noun, but is made up of many "nations."

The book, "The Seven Virgins" *was* not available in the library.
Here there is only one book, although the title of the book is plural.

6. Specific Amounts are always singular

A plural noun that refers to a specific amount or quantity that is considered as a whole (dozen, hundred, score etc.) requires a singular verb.

Examples:

60 minutes *is* quite a long time.
Here "60 minutes" is considered a whole, and therefore one item (singular noun).

The first million is the most difficult.

7. Either, Neither and Each are always singular

The verb is always singular when used with: either, each, neither, every one and many.

Examples:

Either of the boys *is* lying.
Each of the employees *has* been well compensated
Many a police officer *has* been found to be courageous
Every one of the teachers *is* responsible

8. Linking with Either, Or, and Neither match the second subject

Two subjects linked by "either," "or," "nor" or "neither" should have a verb that matches the second subject.
Examples:
Neither David nor Paul *will* be coming.
Either Mary or Tina *is* paying.

Note
If one subject linked by "either," "or," "nor" or "neither" is in plural form, then the verb should also be in plural, and the verb should be close to the plural subject.

Examples:
Neither the mother *nor* her kids *have* eaten.
Either Mary *or* her *friends are* paying.

9. Collective Nouns are Plural

Some collective nouns such as poultry, gentry, cattle, vermin etc. are considered plural and require a plural verb.

Examples:

The *poultry are* sick.
The *cattle are* well fed.

Note

Collective nouns involving people can work with both plural and singular verbs.

Examples:

Nigerians are known to be hard working
Europeans live in Africa

10. Nouns that are Singular and Plural

Nouns like deer, sheep, swine, salmon etc. can be singular or plural and require the same verb form.

Examples:

The swine is feeding. (singular)
The swine are feeding. (plural)

The salmon is on the table. (singular)
The salmon are running upstream. (plural)

11. Collective Nouns are Singular

Collective nouns such as Army, Jury, Assembly, Committee, Team etc should carry a singular verb when they subscribe to one idea. If the ideas or views are more than one, then the verb used should be plural.

Examples:

The committee is in agreement in their decision.

The committee were in disagreement in their decision.
The jury has agreed on a verdict.
The jury were unable to agree on a verdict.

12. Subjects links by "and" are plural.

Two subjects linked by "and" always require a plural verb

Examples:

David and John are students.

Note
If the subjects linked by "and" are used as one phrase, or constitute one idea, then the verb must be singular

The color of his socks and shoe is black.
Here "socks and shoe" are two nouns, however the subject is "color" which is singular.

Help with Building your Vocabulary

Vocabulary tests can be daunting when you think of the enormous number of words that might come up in the exam. As the exam date draws near, your anxiety will grow because you know that no matter how many words you memorize, chances are, you will still remember so few. Here are some tips which you can use to hurdle the big words that may come up in your exam without having to open the dictionary and memorize all the words known to humankind.

Build up and tear apart the big words. Big words, like many other things, are composed of small parts. Some words are made up of many other words. A man who lifts weights for example, is a weight lifter. Words are also made up of word parts called prefixes, suffixes and roots. Often times, we can see the relationship of different words through these parts. A person who is skilled with both hands is ambidextrous. A word with double meaning is ambiguous. A person with two conflicting emotions is ambivalent. Two words with synonymous meanings often have the same root. Bio, a root word derived from Latin is used in words like biography meaning to write about a person's life, and biology meaning the study of living organisms.

- **Words with double meanings.** Did you know that the word husband not only means a man married to a woman, but also thrift or frugality? Sometimes, words have double meanings. The dictionary meaning, or the denotation of a word is sometimes different from the way we use it or its connotation.

- **Read widely, read deeply and read daily.** The best way to expand your vocabulary is to familiarize yourself with as many words as possible through reading. By reading, you are able to remember words in a proper context and thus, remember its meaning or at the very least, its use. Reading widely would help you get acquainted with words you may never use every day. This is the best strategy without doubt. However, if you are studying for an exam next week, or even tomorrow, it isn't much help! Below you will find a range of different ways to learn new words quickly and efficiently.

- **Remember.** Always remember that big words are easy to understand when divided into smaller parts, and the smaller words will often have several other meanings aside from the one you already know. Here are suggested effective ways to help you improve your vocabulary.

- **Be Committed To Learning New Words**. To improve your vocabulary you need to make a commitment to learn new words. Commit to learning at least a word or two a day. You can also get new words by reading books, poems, stories, plays and magazines. Expose yourself to more language to increase the number of new words that you learn.

  - **Learn Practical Vocabulary**. As much as possible, learn vocabulary that is associated with what you do and that you can use regularly. For example learn words related to your profession or hobby. Learn as much vocabulary as you can in your favorite subjects.

  - **Use New Words Frequently**. When you learn a new word start using it and do so frequently. Repeat it when you are alone and try to use the word as often as you can with people you talk to. You can also use flash-cards to practice new words that you learn.

- **Learn the Proper Usage.** If you do not understand the proper usage, look it up and make sure you have it right.

- **Use a Dictionary.** When reading textbooks, novels or assigned readings, keep the dictionary nearby. Also learn how to use online dictionaries and WORD dictionary. When you come across a new word, check its meaning. If you cannot do so immediately, then you should write it down and check it when possible. This will help you understand what the word means and exactly how best to use it.

- **Learn Word Roots, Prefixes and Suffixes.** English words are usually derived from suffixes, prefixes and roots, which come from Latin, French or Greek. Learning the root or origin of a word helps you easily understand the meaning of the word and other words that are derived from the root. Generally, if you learn the meaning of one root word, you will understand two or three words. This is a great two-for-one strategy. Most prefixes, suffixes, roots and stems are used in two, three or more words, so if you know the root, prefix or suffix, you can guess the meaning of many words.

- **Synonyms and Antonyms.** Most words in the English language have two or three (at least) synonyms and antonyms. For example, "big," in the most common usage, has about seventy-five synonyms and an equal number of antonyms. Understanding the relationships between these words and how they all fit together gives your brain a framework, which makes them easier to learn, remember and recall.

- **Use Flash Cards.** Flash cards are one of the best ways to memorize things. They can be used anywhere and anytime, so you can make use of odd free moments waiting for the bus or waiting in line. Make your own or buy commercially prepared flash cards, and keep them with you all the time.

- **Make word lists.** Learning vocabulary, like learning many things, requires repetition. Keep a new words journal in a separate section or separate notebook. Add any words that you look up in the dictionary, as well as from word lists. Review your word lists regularly.

Photocopying or printing off word lists from the Internet or handouts is not the same. Actually writing out the word and a few notes on the definition is an important process for imprinting the word in your brain. Writing out the word and definition in your New Word Journal, forces you to concentrate and focus on the new word. Hitting PRINT or pushing the button on the photocopier does not do the same thing.

Practice Test Questions Set 1

The questions below are not the same as you will find on the TABE® - that would be too easy! And nobody knows what the questions will be and they change all the time. Below are general questions that cover the same subject areas as the TABE®. So, while the format and exact wording of the questions may differ slightly, and change from year to year, if you can answer the questions below, you will have no problem with the TABE®.

For the best results, take these Practice Test Questions as if it were the real exam. Set aside time when you will not be disturbed, and a location that is quiet and free of distractions. Read the instructions carefully, read each question carefully, and answer to the best of your ability.
Use the bubble answer sheets provided. When you have completed the Practice Questions, check your answer against the Answer Key and read the explanation provided.

Do not attempt more than one set of practice test questions in one day. After completing the first practice test, wait two or three days before attempting the second set of questions.

Reading

	A	B	C	D	E		A	B	C	D	E
1	○	○	○	○	○	21	○	○	○	○	○
2	○	○	○	○	○	22	○	○	○	○	○
3	○	○	○	○	○	23	○	○	○	○	○
4	○	○	○	○	○	24	○	○	○	○	○
5	○	○	○	○	○	25	○	○	○	○	○
6	○	○	○	○	○						
7	○	○	○	○	○						
8	○	○	○	○	○						
9	○	○	○	○	○						
10	○	○	○	○	○						
11	○	○	○	○	○						
12	○	○	○	○	○						
13	○	○	○	○	○						
14	○	○	○	○	○						
15	○	○	○	○	○						
16	○	○	○	○	○						
17	○	○	○	○	○						
18	○	○	○	○	○						
19	○	○	○	○	○						
20	○	○	○	○	○						

Computational Mathematics

	A	B	C	D	E			A	B	C	D	E
1	○	○	○	○	○		21	○	○	○	○	○
2	○	○	○	○	○		22	○	○	○	○	○
3	○	○	○	○	○		23	○	○	○	○	○
4	○	○	○	○	○		24	○	○	○	○	○
5	○	○	○	○	○		25	○	○	○	○	○
6	○	○	○	○	○							
7	○	○	○	○	○							
8	○	○	○	○	○							
9	○	○	○	○	○							
10	○	○	○	○	○							
11	○	○	○	○	○							
12	○	○	○	○	○							
13	○	○	○	○	○							
14	○	○	○	○	○							
15	○	○	○	○	○							
16	○	○	○	○	○							
17	○	○	○	○	○							
18	○	○	○	○	○							
19	○	○	○	○	○							
20	○	○	○	○	○							

Applied Mathematics

	A	B	C	D	E		A	B	C	D	E
1	○	○	○	○	○	21	○	○	○	○	○
2	○	○	○	○	○	22	○	○	○	○	○
3	○	○	○	○	○	23	○	○	○	○	○
4	○	○	○	○	○	24	○	○	○	○	○
5	○	○	○	○	○	25	○	○	○	○	○
6	○	○	○	○	○						
7	○	○	○	○	○						
8	○	○	○	○	○						
9	○	○	○	○	○						
10	○	○	○	○	○						
11	○	○	○	○	○						
12	○	○	○	○	○						
13	○	○	○	○	○						
14	○	○	○	○	○						
15	○	○	○	○	○						
16	○	○	○	○	○						
17	○	○	○	○	○						
18	○	○	○	○	○						
19	○	○	○	○	○						
20	○	○	○	○	○						

Language

	A	B	C	D	E		A	B	C	D	E
1	○	○	○	○	○	21	○	○	○	○	○
2	○	○	○	○	○	22	○	○	○	○	○
3	○	○	○	○	○	23	○	○	○	○	○
4	○	○	○	○	○	24	○	○	○	○	○
5	○	○	○	○	○	25	○	○	○	○	○
6	○	○	○	○	○	26	○	○	○	○	○
7	○	○	○	○	○	27	○	○	○	○	○
8	○	○	○	○	○	28	○	○	○	○	○
9	○	○	○	○	○	29	○	○	○	○	○
10	○	○	○	○	○	30	○	○	○	○	○
11	○	○	○	○	○	31	○	○	○	○	○
12	○	○	○	○	○	32	○	○	○	○	○
13	○	○	○	○	○	33	○	○	○	○	○
14	○	○	○	○	○	34	○	○	○	○	○
15	○	○	○	○	○	35	○	○	○	○	○
16	○	○	○	○	○	36	○	○	○	○	○
17	○	○	○	○	○	37	○	○	○	○	○
18	○	○	○	○	○	38	○	○	○	○	○
19	○	○	○	○	○	39	○	○	○	○	○
20	○	○	○	○	○	40	○	○	○	○	○

Reading and Language Arts

Directions: The following questions are based on several reading passages. A series of questions follow each passage. Read each passage carefully, and then answer the questions based on it. You may reread the passage as often as you wish. When you have finished answering the questions based on one passage, go right onto the next passage. Choose the best answer based on the information given and implied.

Questions 1 – 4 refer to the following passage.

Passage 1 - The Life of Helen Keller

Many people have heard of Helen Keller. She is famous because she was unable to see or hear, but learned to speak and read and went onto attend college and earn a degree. Her life is a very interesting story, one that she developed into an autobiography, which was then adapted into both a stage play and a movie. How did Helen Keller overcome her disabilities to become a famous woman? Read on to find out. Helen Keller was not born blind and deaf. When she was a small baby, she had a very high fever for several days. As a result of her sudden illness, baby Helen lost her eyesight and her hearing. Because she was so young when she went deaf and blind, Helen Keller never had any recollection of being able to see or hear. Since she could not hear, she could not learn to talk. Since she could not see, it was difficult for her to move around. For the first six years of her life, her world was very still and dark.

Imagine what Helen's childhood was like. She could not hear her mother's voice. She could not see the beauty of her parent's farm. She could not recognize who was giving her a hug, or a bath or even where her bedroom was each night. Worse, she could not communicate with her parents in any way. She could not express her feelings or tell them the things she wanted. It must have been a very sad childhood.

When Helen was six years old, her parents hired her a teacher named Anne Sullivan. Anne was a young woman who was almost blind. However, she could hear and she could read Braille, so she was a perfect teacher for young Helen. At first, Anne had a very hard time teaching Helen anything. She described her first impression of Helen as a "wild thing, not a child." Helen did not like Anne at first either. She bit and hit Anne when Anne tried to teach her. However, the two of them eventually came to have a great deal of love and respect.

Anne taught Helen to hear by putting her hands on people's throats. She could feel the sounds people made. In time, Helen learned to feel what people said. Next, Anne taught Helen to read Braille, which is a way that books are written for the blind. Finally, Anne taught Helen to talk. Although Helen did learn to talk, it was hard for anyone but Anne to understand her.

As Helen grew older, she amazed more and more people with her story. She went to college and wrote books about her life. She gave talks to the public, with Anne at her side, translating her words. Today, both Anne Sullivan and Helen Keller are famous women who are respected for their lives' work.

1. Helen Keller could not see and hear and so, what was her biggest problem in childhood?

    a. Inability to communicate

    b. Inability to walk

    c. Inability to play

    d. Inability to eat

2. Helen learned to hear by feeling the vibrations people made when they spoke. What were these vibrations were felt through?

    a. Mouth

    b. Throat

    c. Ears

    d. Lips

3. From the passage, we can infer that Anne Sullivan was a patient teacher. We can infer this because

a. Helen hit and bit her and Anne remained her teacher.

b. Anne taught Helen to read only.

c. Anne was hard of hearing too.

d. Anne wanted to be a teacher.

4. Helen Keller learned to speak but Anne translated her words when she spoke in public. The reason Helen needed a translator was because

a. Helen spoke another language.

b. Helen's words were hard for people to understand.

c. Helen spoke very quietly.

d. Helen did not speak but only used sign language.

Questions 5 – 7 refer to the following passage.

Passage 2 - Ways Characters Communicate in Theater

Playwrights give their characters voices in a way that gives depth and added meaning to what happens on stage during their play. There are different types of speech in scripts that allow characters to talk with themselves, with other characters, and even with the audience.

It is very unique to theater that characters may talk "to themselves." When characters do this, the speech they give is called a soliloquy. Soliloquies are usually poetic, introspective, moving, and can tell audience members about the feelings, motivations, or suspicions of an individual character without that character having to reveal them to other characters on stage. "To be or not to be" is a famous soliloquy given by Hamlet as he considers difficult but important themes, such as life and death.

The most common type of communication in plays is when one character is speaking to another or a group of other characters. This is generally called dialogue, but can also be called monologue if one character speaks without being interrupted for a long time. It is not necessarily the most important type of communication, but it is the most common because the plot of the play cannot really progress without it.

Lastly, and most unique to theater (although it has been used somewhat in film) is when a character speaks directly to the audience. This is called an aside, and scripts usually specifically direct actors to do this. Asides are usually comical, an inside joke between the character and the audience, and very short. The actor will usually face the audience when delivering them, even if it's for a moment, so the audience can recognize this move as an aside.

All three of these types of communication are important to the art of theater, and have been perfected by famous playwrights like Shakespeare. Understanding these types of communication can help an audience member grasp what is artful about the script and action of a play.

5. According to the passage, characters in plays communicate to

    a. move the plot forward

    b. show the private thoughts and feelings of one character

    c. make the audience laugh

    d. add beauty and artistry to the play

6. When Hamlet delivers "To be or not to be," he can most likely be described as

    a. solitary

    b. thoughtful

    c. dramatic

    d. hopeless

7. The author uses parentheses to punctuate "although it has been used somewhat in film,"

    a. to show that films are less important

    b. instead of using commas so that the sentence is not interrupted

    c. because parenthesis help separate details that are not as important

    d. to show that films are not as artistic

Questions 8 – 10 refer to the following passage.

Passage 3 - Low Blood Sugar

As the name suggest, low blood sugar is low sugar levels in the bloodstream. This can occur when you have not eaten properly and undertake strenuous activity, or, when you are very hungry. When Low blood sugar occurs regularly and is ongoing, it is a medical condition called hypoglycemia. This condition can occur in diabetics and in healthy adults.

Causes of low blood sugar can include excessive alcohol consumption, metabolic problems, stomach surgery, pancreas, liver or kidneys problems, as well as a side-effect of some medications.

Symptoms

There are different symptoms depending on the severity of the case.

Mild hypoglycemia can lead to feelings of nausea and hunger. The patient may also feel nervous, jittery and have fast heart beats. Sweaty skin, clammy and cold skin are likely symptoms.
Moderate hypoglycemia can result in a short temper, confusion, nervousness, fear and blurring of vision. The patient may feel weak and unsteady.

Severe cases of hypoglycemia can lead to seizures, coma, fainting spells, nightmares, headaches, excessive sweats and severe tiredness.

Diagnosis of low blood sugar

A doctor can diagnosis this medical condition by asking the patient questions and testing blood and urine samples. Home testing kits are available for patients to monitor blood sugar levels. It is important to see a qualified doctor though. The doctor can administer tests to ensure that will safely rule out other medical conditions that could affect blood sugar levels.

Treatment

Quick treatments include drinking or eating foods and drinks with high sugar contents. Good examples include soda, fruit juice, hard candy and raisins. Glucose energy tablets can also help. Doctors may also recommend medications and well as changes in diet and exercise routine to treat chronic low blood sugar.

8. Based on the article, which of the following is true?

    a. Low blood sugar can happen to anyone.

    b. Low blood sugar only happens to diabetics.

    c. Low blood sugar can occur even.

    d. None of the statements are true.

9. Which of the following are the author's opinion?

    a. Quick treatments include drinking or eating foods and drinks with high sugar contents.

    b. None of the statements are opinions.

    c. This condition can occur in diabetics and also in healthy adults.

    d. There are different symptoms depending on the severity of the case

10. What is the author's purpose?

   a. To inform

   b. To persuade

   c. To entertain

   d. To analyze

11. Which of the following is not a detail?

   a. A doctor can diagnosis this medical condition by asking the patient questions and testing.

   b. A doctor will test blood and urine samples.

   c. Glucose energy tablets can also help.

   d. Home test kits monitor blood sugar levels.

   d. None of the above.

Questions 12 – 15 refer to the following passage.

How To Get A Good Nights Sleep

Sleep is just as essential for healthy living as water, air and food. Sleep allows the body to rest and replenish depleted energy levels. Sometimes we may, for various reasons, have trouble sleeping which has a serious effect on our health. Those who have prolonged sleeping problems are facing a serious medical condition and should see a qualified doctor when possible for help. Here is simple guide that can help you sleep better at night.

Try to create a natural pattern of waking up and sleeping around the same time every day. This means avoiding going to bed too early and oversleeping past your usual wake up time. Going to bed and getting up at radically different times everyday confuses your body clock. Try to establish a natural rhythm as much as you can.

Exercises and a bit of physical activity can help you sleep

better at night. If you are having problem sleeping, try to be as active as you can during the day. If you are tired from physical activity, falling asleep is a natural and easy process for your body. If you remain inactive during the day, you will find it harder to sleep properly at night. Try walking, jogging, swimming or simple stretches as you get close to your bed time.

Afternoon naps are great to refresh you during the day, but they may also keep you awake at night. If you feel sleepy during the day, get up, take a walk and get busy to keep from sleeping. Stretching is a good way to increase blood flow to the brain and keep you alert so that you don't sleep during the day. This will help you sleep better night.

> A warm bath or a glass of milk in the evening can help your body relax and prepare for sleep. A cold bath will wake you up and keep you up for several hours. Also avoid eating too late before bed.

12. How would you describe this sentence?

   a. A recommendation

   b. An opinion

   c. A fact

   d. A diagnosis

13. Which of the following is an alternative title for this article?

   a. Exercise and a good night's sleep

   b. Benefits of a good night's sleep

   c. Tips for a good night's sleep

   d. Lack of sleep is a serious medical condition

14. Which of the following cannot be inferred from this article?

   a. Biking is helpful for getting a good night's sleep
   b. Mental activity is helpful for getting a good night's sleep
   c. Eating bedtime snacks is not recommended
   d. Getting up at the same time is helpful for a good night's sleep

15. What is a disadvantage of taking naps?

   a. They may keep you awake.
   b. There are no disadvantages
   c. They may help you sleep better
   d. They may affect your diet

Question 16 refers to the following Table of Contents.

Contents

    Science Self-assessment 81
    Answer Key 91
    Science Tutorials 96
    Scientific Method 96
    Biology 99
    Heredity: Genes and Mutation 104
    Classification 108
    Ecology 110
    Chemistry 112
    Energy: Kinetic and Mechanical 126
    Energy: Work and Power 130
    Force: Newton's Three Laws 132

16. Consider the table of contents above. What page would you find information about natural selection and adaptation?

    a. 81
    b. 90
    c. 110
    d. 132

Questions 17 – 19 refer to the following passage.

Passage 5 - Pearl Harbor

A Day That Will Live in Infamy! Attack on Pearl Harbor
In 1941, the world was at war. The United States was trying very hard to keep itself out of the conflict. In Europe, the countries of Germany and Italy had formed an alliance to expand their land and territory. Germany had already taken over Poland, Denmark, and parts of France. They were heading next toward England and due to all the fighting in Europe, there were battles taking place as far south as North Africa, where the German and Italian armies were fighting the British.

This got even worse when the Asian nation of Japan formed an alliance with Germany and Italy. Together, the three countries called themselves, the AXIS. Now, the war was in the Pacific as well as in Europe and Northern Africa. A great deal of Americans felt that perhaps now was the time for the United States to join with its ally, Great Britain and stop the Axis from taking over more regions of the world.

In 1941, Franklin Roosevelt was President of the United States. His fear at the time was that Japan would try to take over many countries in Asia. He did not want to see that happen, so he moved some of the United States warships that had been stationed in San Diego, to the military base at Pearl Harbor, in Honolulu, Hawaii.

Japan quietly plotted their attack. They waited until the early hours of the morning on Sunday, December 7, 1941.

Then, 350 Japanese war plans began to drop bombs on the U.S. ships at Pearl Harbor. The first bombs fell at 7:48 am and a mere 90 minutes later, the attack was over. Pearl Harbor was decimated. 8 battleships were damaged. Eleven ships were sunk and 300 U.S. planes were destroyed. Most devastating was the loss of life 2,400 U.S. military members was killed in the attack and 1, 282 were injured.

President Roosevelt addressed the country via the radio and said "Today is a day that will live in infamy." He asked Congress to declare war on Japan. War was declared on Japan on December 8th and on Germany and Italy on December 11th. The United States had entered World War Two.

17. After reading the passage, what can we infer infamy means?

    a. Famous

    b. Remembered in a good way

    c. Remembered in a bad way

    d. Easily forgotten

18. What three countries formed the Axis?

    a. Italy, England, Germany

    b. United States, England, Italy

    c. Germany, Japan, Italy

    d. Germany, Japan, United States

19. What do you think was President Roosevelt's reason for moving warships to Pearl Harbor?

    a. He feared Japan would bomb San Diego

    b. He knew Japan was going to attack Pearl Harbor

    c. He was planning to attack Japan

    d. He wanted to try and protect Asian countries from Japanese takeover

20. Why do you think Japan chose a Sunday morning at 7:48 am for their attack?

   a. They knew the military slept late

   b. There is a law against bombing countries on a Sunday

   c. They wanted the attack to catch people by surprise

   d. That was the only free time they had to attack.

Questions 21 - 24 refer to the following recipe.

If You Have Allergies, You're Not Alone

People who experience allergies might joke that their immune systems have let them down or are seriously lacking. Truthfully though, people who experience allergic reactions or allergy symptoms during certain times of the year have heightened immune systems that are, "better" than those of people who have perfectly healthy but less militant immune systems.

Still, when a person has an allergic reaction, they are having an adverse reaction to a substance that is considered normal to most people. Mild allergic reactions usually have symptoms like itching, runny nose, red eyes, or bumps or discoloration of the skin. More serious allergic reactions, such as those to animal and insect poisons or certain foods, may result in the closing of the throat, swelling of the eyes, low blood pressure, inability to breath, and can even be fatal.

Different treatments help different allergies, and which one a person uses depends on the nature and severity of the allergy. It is recommended to patients with severe allergies to take extra precautions, such as carrying an EpiPen, which treats anaphylactic shock and may prevent death, always in order for the remedy to be readily available and more effective. When an allergy is not so severe, treatments may be used just relieve a person of uncomfortable symptoms. Over the counter allergy medicines treat milder symptoms, and can be bought at any grocery store and used in moderation to help people with allergies live normally.

There are many tests available to assess whether a person has allergies or what they may be allergic to, and advances in these tests and the medicine used to treat patients continues to improve. Despite this fact, allergies still affect many people throughout the year or even every day. Medicines used to treat allergies have side effects of their own, and it is difficult to bring the body into balance with the use of medicine. Regardless, many of those who live with allergies are grateful for what is available and find it useful in maintaining their lifestyles.

21. According to this passage, the word that the word "militant" belongs in a group with the words:

    a. sickly, ailing, faint

    b. strength, power, vigor

    c. active, fighting, warring

    d. worn, tired, breaking down

22. The author says that "medicines used to treat allergies have side-effects of their own" to

    a. point out that doctors aren't very good at diagnosing and treating allergies

    b. argue that because of the large number of people with allergies, a cure will never be found

    c. explain that allergy medicines aren't cures and some compromise must be made

    d. argue that more wholesome remedies should be researched and medicines banned

23. It can be inferred that _____ recommend that some people with allergies carry medicine with them.

    a. the author

    b. doctors

    c. the makers of EpiPen

    d. people with allergies

24. The author has written this passage to

   a. inform readers on symptoms of allergies so people with allergies can get help

   b. persuade readers to be proud of having allergies

   c. inform readers on different remedies so people with allergies receive the right help

   d. describe different types of allergies, their symptoms, and their remedies

Questions 25 – 26 refer to the following email.

SUBJECT: MEDICAL STAFF CHANGES

To all staff:

This email is to advise you of a paper on recommended medical staff changes has been posted to the Human Resources website.

The contents are of primary interest to medical staff, other staff may be interested in reading it, particularly those in medical support roles.

The paper deals with several major issues:

   1. Improving our ability to attract top quality staff to the hospital, and retain our existing staff. These changes will make our position and departmental names internationally recognizable and comparable with North American and North Asian departments and positions.

   2. Improving our ability to attract top quality staff by introducing greater flexibility in the departmental structure.

   3. General comments on issues to be further discussed in relation to research staff.

The changes outlined in this paper are significant. I encourage you to read the document and send to me any comments you may have, so that it can be enhanced and improved.

Gordon Simms
Administrator,
Seven Oaks Regional Hospital

25. Are all hospital staff required to read the document posted to the Human Resources website?

    a. Yes all staff are required to read the document.

    b. No, reading the document is optional.

    c. Only medical staff are required to read the document.

    d. none of the above are correct.

Computational Mathematics

1. What fraction of $1500 is $75?

    a. 1/14

    b. 3/5

    c. 7/10

    d. 1/20

2. Estimate 215 x 65.

    a. 1,350

    b. 13,500

    c. 103,500

    d. 3,500

3. Below is the attendance for a class of 45.

Day	Number of Absent Students
Monday	5
Tuesday	9
Wednesday	4
Thursday	10
Friday	6

What is the average attendance for the week?

    a. 88%
    b. 85%
    c. 81%
    d. 77%

4. 2/3 − 2/5 =

    a. 4/10
    b. 1/15
    c. 3/7
    d. 4/15

5. **Express 0.27 + 0.33 as a fraction.**

    a. 3/6
    b. 4/7
    c. 3/5
    d. 2/7

6. $7^5 - 3^5 =$

    a. 15,000
    b. 16,564
    c. 15,800
    d. 15,007

7. What is 2/4 X 3/4 reduced to lowest terms?

    a. 6/12
    b. 3/8
    c. 6/16
    d. 3/4

8. Solve the following equation 4(y + 6) = 3y + 30

    a. y = 20
    b. y = 6
    c. y = 30/7
    d. y = 30

9. 2/3 of 60 + 1/5 of 75 =

    a. 45
    b. 55
    c. 15
    d. 50

10. What is 1/3 of 3/4?

    a. 1/4
    b. 1/3
    c. 2/3
    d. 3/4

11. What is (3.13 + 7.87) X 5?

    a. 65
    b. 50
    c. 45
    d. 55

12. Express 5 x 5 x 5 x 5 x 5 x 5 in exponential form.

    a. 5^6
    b. 10^6
    c. 5^{16}
    d. 5^3

13. Express 9 x 9 x 9 in exponential form and standard form.

    a. $9^3 = 719$
    b. $9^3 = 629$
    c. $9^3 = 729$
    d. $10^3 = 729$

14. If y = 4 and x = 3, solve yx^3

    a. -108
    b. 108
    c. 27
    d. 4

15. Divide 0.524 by 10^3

    a. 0.0524
    b. 0.000524
    c. 0.00524
    d. 524

16. Solve 3x − 27 = 0

    a. x = 24
    b. x = 30
    c. x = 9
    d. x = 21

17. Which of the following is between 7/11 and 5/7?

    a. 0.6
    b. 13/17
    c. 2/3
    d. 11/15

18. Solve: 0.25 + 0.65

    a. 1/2
    b. 9/10
    c. 4/7
    d. 2/9

19. 389 + 454 =

    a. 853
    b. 833
    c. 843
    d. 863

20. 9,177 + 7,204 =

    a. 16,4712
    b. 16,371
    c. 16,381
    d. 15,412

21. 2,199 + 5,832 =

    a. 8,331
    b. 8,041
    c. 8,141
    d. 8,031

22. 8,390 - 5,239 =

    a. 3,261
    b. 3,151
    c. 3,161
    d. 3,101

23. 643 - 587 =

    a. 56
    b. 66
    c. 46
    d. 55

24. 3,406 - 2,767 =

    a. 629
    b. 720
    c. 639
    d. 649

25. 149 × 7 =

    a. 1032
    b. 1043
    c. 1059
    d. 1063

Applied Mathematics

1. A square box measures 20 cm long and 20 cm wide and 20 cm high. What is the volume of the box?

    a. 60 cm³
    b. 20,000 cm³
    c. 4,000 cm³
    d. 8,000 cm³

2. A worker's weekly salary was increased by 30%. If his new salary is $150, what was his old salary?

    a. $120.00
    b. $99.15
    c. $109.00
    d. $115.40

3. Mr. Jones runs a factory. His total assets are $256,800 which consists of a building worth $80,500, machinery worth $125.000 and $51,300 cash. After one year what will be the value of his total assets if he has additional cash of $75,600 and the value of his building has increased by 10% per year, and his machinery depreciated by 20%?

    a. $243,450
    b. $252,450
    c. $315,450
    d. $272,350

4. Brad has agreed to buy everyone a Coke. Each drink costs $1.89, and there are 5 friends. Estimate Brad's cost.

   a. $7
   b. $8
   c. $10
   d. $12

5. The manager of a weaving factory estimates that if 10 machines run at 100% efficiency for 8 hours, they will produce 1450 meters of cloth. Due to some technical problems, 4 machines run of 95% efficiency and the remaining 6 at 90% efficiency. How many meters of cloth can these machines will produce in 8 hours?

   a. 1334 meters
   b. 1310 meters
   c. 1300 meters
   d. 1285 meters

6. My current pay is 'x' dollars. Every month it is increased 0.5%. After 'y' months, what will my pay be?

   a. X + 0.005xy
   b. 1.002xy
   c. X + 1.005xy/y
   d. X + 1.005xy

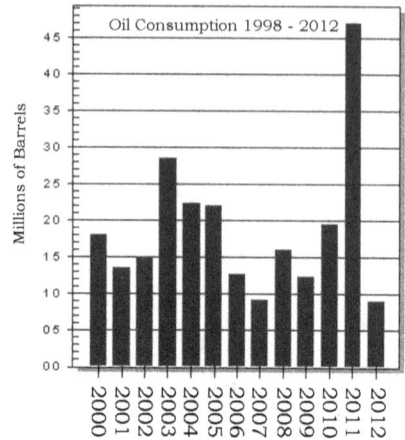

7. The graph above shows oil consumption in millions of barrels for the period, 1998 - 2012. What year did oil consumption peak?

    a. 2011
    b. 2010
    c. 2008
    d. 2009

8. In a local election at polling station A, 945 voters cast their vote out of 1270 registered voters. At polling station B, 860 cast their vote out of 1050 registered voters and at station C, 1210 cast their vote out of 1440 registered voters. What is the total turnout from all three polling stations?

    a. 70%
    b. 74%
    c. 76%
    d. 80%

9. A pet store sold $19,304.56 worth of merchandise in June. If the cost of products sold was $5,284.34, employees were paid $8,384.76, and rent was $2,920.00, how much profit did the store make in June?

   a. $5,635.46
   b. $2,714.46
   c. $14,020.22
   d. $10,019.80
   e) $16,383.57

10. A small lot has a perimeter of 100 feet. What's the area, expressed in square feet?

   a. We cannot tell from this information.
   b. 10 ft^2
   c. 400 ft^2
   d. 25 ft^2

11. John is a barber and receives 40% of the amount paid by each of his customers. John gets all of any tips paid to him. If a customer pays $8.50 for a haircut and pays a tip of $1.30, how much money goes to John?

   a. $3.92
   b. $4.70
   c. $5.30
   d. $6.40

12. Mr. Jones bought 5 children's tickets and 9 adult tickets to the zoo. He paid a total of $67. Mr. Jackson paid $38.50 for 7 adult tickets. What is the cost of each type of ticket?

a. adult = $13.40 and children = $47.44
b. adult = $7.44 and children = $13.40
c. adult = $3.50 and children = $5.50
d. adult = $5.50 and children = $3.50

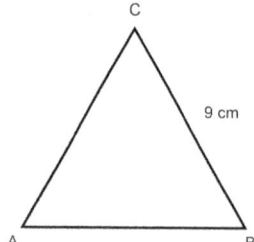

13. What is the perimeter of the equilateral △ABC above?

a. 18 cm
b. 12 cm
c. 27 cm
d. 15 cm

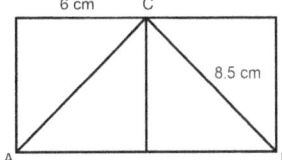

Note: Figure not drawn to scale

14. Assuming the 2 quadrangles above are identical rectangles, what is the perimeter of △ABC in the above shape?

    a. 25.5 cm
    b. 27 cm
    c. 30 cm
    d. 29 cm

15. A woman spent 15% of her income on an item and ends up with $120. What percentage of her income is left?

    a. 12%
    b. 85%
    c. 75%
    d. 95%

16. A rectangular box measures 10 cm long and 8 cm wide and 10 cm high. What is the volume of the box?

    a. 28 cm³
    b. 2000 cm³
    c. 400 cm³
    d. 800 cm³

17. At the beginning of 2009, Marilyn invested $5,000 in a savings account. The account pays 4% interest per year. At the end 2 years, how much did Marilyn have in the account?

    a. $5,200
    b. $5,408
    c. $5,110
    d. $7,000

18. A distributor purchased 550 kilograms of potatoes for $165. He distributed these at a rate of $6.4 per 20 kilograms to 15 shops, $3.4 per 10 kilograms to 12 shops and the remainder at $1.8 per 5 kilograms. If his total distribution cost is $10, what will his profit be?

    a. $10.4
    b. $13.6
    c. $14.9
    d. $23.4

19. A car covers a distance in 3.5 hours with an average speed of 60 km/hr. How much time in hours will a motorbike take to cover this distance with average speed of 40km/hr?

    a. 6 hours
    b. 5 hours
    c. 5.5 hours
    d. 5.25 hours

20. Write 51.738 to the nearest 100th.

    a. 51.735
    b. 51.7
    c. 51.73
    d. 51.74

21. What is the ratio between 2 gold coins, 6 silver coins and 12 bronze coins?

   a. 2:3:4
   b. 1:2:4
   c. 1:3:6
   d. 2:3:4

22. Choose the expression the figure represents.

   a. X < 1
   b. X < 1
   c. X > 1
   d. X ≠ 1

23. Choose the expression the figure represents.

   a. X > 2
   b. X > 2
   c. X < 2
   d. X ≠ 2

24. Convert 7,892,000,000 to scientific notation.

    a. 7.892×10^{10}
    b. 7.892×10^{-9}
    c. 7.892×10^{9}
    d. 0.7892×10^{11}

25. Consider the following sequence:

+ * + * | * + * + | * * + * | + + __ __

    a. + *
    b. * *
    c. + +
    d. * +

English

For questions 1 - 5, fill in the blank with the correct punctuation.

1. Watch out for the broken glass ____

    a. .
    b. ?
    c. ,
    d. !

2. We saw many beautiful sights on our vacation____ but we spent too many hours on the road.

    a. ,
    b. :
    c. ;
    d. .

3. She loved fresh vegetables at dinner _____ he wanted only meat on his dinner table.

    a. ,
    b. :
    c. ;
    d. .

4. Cautiously, he investigated the noise _____ but it was only the cat scratching the door.

    a. !
    b. :
    c. ;
    d. .

5. We packed a tent, several sleeping bags, a stove _____ and plenty of foods.

    a. ,
    b. :
    c. ;
    d. .

6. Choose the sentence below with the correct punctuation.

    a. George wrecked John's car that was the end of their friendship.

    b. George wrecked John's car. that was the end of their friendship.

    c. George wrecked John's car; that was the end of their friendship.

    d. None of the above

7. Choose the sentence below with the correct punctuation.

    a. The dress was not Gina's favorite; however, she wore it to the dance.

    b. The dress was not Gina's favorite, however, she wore it to the dance.

    c. The dress was not Gina's favorite, however; she wore it to the dance.

    d. The dress was not Gina's favorite however, she wore it to the dance.

8. Choose the sentence below with the correct punctuation.

    a. Chris showed his dedication to golf in many ways, for example, he watched all the tournaments on television.

    b. Chris showed his dedication to golf in many ways; for example, he watched all the tournaments on television.

    c. Chris showed his dedication to golf in many ways, for example; he watched all the tournaments on television.

    d. Chris showed his dedication to golf in many ways for example he watched all the tournaments on television.

9. Choose the sentence below with the correct punctuation.

    a. There are many species of owls, the Great-Horned Owl, the Snowy Owl, and the Western Screech Owl, and the Barn Owl.

    b. There are many species of owls, the Great-Horned Owl: the Snowy Owl: and the Western Screech Owl, and the Barn Owl.

    c. There are many species of owls; the Great-Horned Owl, the Snowy Owl, and the Western Screech Owl, and the Barn Owl.

    d. There are many species of owls: the Great-Horned Owl, the Snowy Owl, the Western Screech Owl, and the Barn Owl.

10. Choose the sentence below with the correct punctuation.

    a. In his most famous speech, Reverend King proclaimed: "I have a dream!"

    b. In his most famous speech, Reverend King proclaimed; "I have a dream!"

    c. In his most famous speech, Reverend King proclaimed. "I have a dream!"

    d. In his most famous speech: Reverend King proclaimed, "I have a dream!"

11. Choose the sentence with the correct punctuation and capitalization.

    a. "How often do you read the newspaper?" his father asked.

    b. How often do you read the newspaper. His father asked.

    c. "How often do you read the newspaper, his father asked?

    d. How often do you read the newspaper his father asked.

12. Choose the sentence with the correct punctuation and capitalization.

    a. The City of Miami is not the capital of Florida.

    b. Tallahassee has been the capital of florida since 1,824.

    c. Where can I find California's best beaches?

    d. My parents used to live in brooklyn, New York.

13. Choose the sentence with the correct punctuation and capitalization.

a. The Wall street journal and New York times are popular newspapers.

b. I read the Chicago Tribune every day.

c. Mr Smith has the Weekend Newspaper delivered to his home.

d. Usa Today is published by the Gannett Company.

14. Choose the sentence with the correct punctuation and capitalization.

a. The ANB is the bank, the only bank, that I trust with my money.

b. The ANB is the bank; The Only Bank; that I trust with my money.

c. The ANB is the bank the only bank that I trust with my money.

d. The ANB is the bank – the only bank that I trust with my money.

15. Choose the sentence with the correct punctuation and capitalization.

a. John Legend performed "All of Me" at the 2014 Grammys.

b. John Legend performed All of Me at the Grammys.

c. John Legend performed – All of Me – at the Grammys.

d. John Legend Performed "All of me at the 2014 Grammys."

16. Combine the following two sentences into one sentence with the same meaning.

He writes poetry.
He plays sports.

    a. He writes poetry as well as sports.

    b. He writes poetry instead of playing sports.

    c. He not only writes poetry, but also plays sports.

    d. He writes poetry to play sports.

17. Combine the following two sentences into one sentence with the same meaning.

The student was punished.
The student was rude to the teacher.

    a. The student was punished as a result of being rude to the teacher.

    b. Even if the student was rude to the teacher, he was punished.

    c. Because the student was punished, he was rude to the teacher.

    d. The student was rude to the teacher but he was punished.

18. Combine the following two sentences into one sentence with the same meaning.

He failed his exam
He is quite lazy.

    a. He is quite lazy after he failed his exam.

    b. He failed his exam because he is quite lazy.

    c. Although he failed his exam he is quite lazy.

    d. Only if he failed his exam he is quite lazy.

19. Combine the following two sentences into one sentence with the same meaning.

Paolo will not be allowed to go.
Paolo has not completed his chores.

    a. Despite Paolo not completing his chores, he will not be allowed to go.

    b. Paolo has not completed his chores, although he will not be allowed to go.

    c. So that Paolo has not completed his chores, he will not be allowed to go.

    d. If Paolo has not completed his chores, he will not be allowed to go.

20. Combine the following two sentences into one sentence with the same meaning.

My mother picked up her car keys.
My mother plans to drive to the store.

    a. My mother picked up her car keys as she plans to drive to the store.

    b. When my mother plans to drive to the store she pick up her car keys.

    c. Even if my mother picked up her car keys, she plans to drive to the store.

    d. My mother picked up her car keys but she plans to drive to the store.

Directions: For questions 21 - 24 below, you are given a topic sentence. Choose the sentence which best develops the given topic sentence.

21. Acquiring real estate is an important investment.

   a. Interest rates on mortgage are at an all-time low.

   b. Older homes have a certain aesthetic appeal to mature buyers.

   c. This decision should be made only after thorough research.

   d. Banks usual don't give mortgages to unqualified individuals.

22. Taking vacations together helps to strengthen family bonds.

   a. Many families choose to book their flights months in advance.

   b. Travelling by plane is can be expensive and unsafe.

   c. Members return home with a fresh perspective on life.

   d. Children enjoy vacations because it's a time to have fun.

23. Global economic imbalances have contributed to poverty.

   a. 75 percent of America's wealth is controlled by the richest ten percent.

   b. Clean drinking water is scarce in some developing countries.

   c. Many people in the poorest countries die from hunger daily.

   d. Unemployment and illiteracy are on the rise globally.

24. A job interview is a potential employee's chance to make a good impression.

a. Managers sometimes fire employees because of misconduct.

b. A first degree is no longer enough to qualify for certain jobs.

c. Employers usually prefer interviewees with experience.

d. Interviewees are first judged by how they are dressed.

25. Player performance and behavior affect attendance at NBA matches.

a. Michael Jordan is the best basketball player of all time.

b. Disenchanted fans often stay away as a form of protest.

c. Though games are televised, the court side experience is better.

d. The NBA lays out strict rules that players must follow on court.

Questions 26 - 30 refer to the following passage.

Read the passage below and look at the numbered, underlined phrases. Choose the answer that is written correctly for each underlined part.

Insects, like humans, assimilate themselves into communities. Humans, as well as insects (26), divide labor among the individual members, with individuals or members carrying out unique roles, responsibilities or functions. Not all humans are equipt by (27) the same skills. Neither are all insects within the same community or colony. In some colonies the function of some insects are for reproduction (28), others carry out the day to day labor such as collecting food or constructing homes, and still others function as protectors or defenders, ensuring the overall safety of the community. Humans too have their assigned functions within their communities. There are construction workers which provide homes for the rest of the community to dwell in. There are farmers who produce the food to feed the community. There are police, soldiers and security guards that see about the safety of the community. Of course, in human communities, unlike among insects, there is significant overlap in functions. The human who gathers food in the field also builds the home and keeps it safe. However neither male humans nor most male insects, no matter how much they may desire it, are able to take on the reproductive role.

One difference over insect and human communities (29) is the principle of working together for the communal good. Among insect colonies, such as termites and ants, all efforts are united to achieve the community goal. Humans generally don't work together for the common goal, except it involves a job for which they are being paid.

Insects are innately programed to carry out their duties. From observations there is never a sense of being cheated or wanting to advance ahead of the colony into a role of superiority. Television shows may depict human character traits in insects but that's all a farce. Insects do not have the ability to develop those patterns of behavior. Perhaps its high time (30) humans really learn from insects.

26. Choose the correct version.

    a. Humans, moreover insects

    b. Humans, also as insects

    c. Humans, additional insects

    d. Correct as is.

27. Choose the correct version.

    a. humans are equipped with

    b. humans are equipped by

    c. humans are equipt with

    d. Correct as is.

28. Choose the correct version.

a. the function of some insects were for reproduction
b. the functions of some insects is for reproduction
c. the function of some insect is for reproductions
d. Correct as is.

29. Choose the correct version.

a. difference among insect and human communities
b. difference from insect and human communities
c. difference between insect and human communities
d. Correct as is.

30. Choose the correct version.

a. Perhaps it's high time
b. Perhaps it'll be high time
c. Perhaps its' high time
d. Correct as is.

31. When Craig's dog was struck by a car, he rushed his pet to the _____.

a. Emergency room
b. Doctor
c. Veterinarian
d. Podiatrist

32. After she received her influenza vaccination, Nan thought that she was _____ to the common cold.

a. Immune
b. Susceptible
c. Vulnerable
d. At risk

33. Paul's rose bushes were being destroyed by Japanese beetles, so he invested in a good _____.

    a. Fungicide
    b. Fertilizer
    c. Sprinkler
    d. Pesticide

34. The last time that the crops failed, the entire nation experienced months of _____.

    a. Famine
    b. Harvest
    c. Plentitude
    d. Disease

35. Because of a pituitary dysfunction, Karl lacked the necessary _____ to grow as tall as his father.

    a. Glands
    b. Hormones
    c. Vitamins
    d. Testosterone

For questions 36 - 40, choose the word that best completes both sentences.

36. He never agrees with his political party. He has a reputation as a _____.

Her reputation as a _____ often gets her into trouble.

    a. Maverick
    b. Conformist
    c. Insider
    d. None of the above

37. With 8 kids, their house is always _____.

The 50% off sale was _____.

    a. Noisy
    b. Orderly
    c. Pandemonium
    d. None of the above

38. The water slowly _____ into the earth.

Don't worry it will _____ in a few minutes.

    a. Degenerate
    b. Dissipate
    c. Scatter
    d. None of the above

39. His skinny frame and _____ face scared me.

His eyes were sunken and his face was _____ .

    a. Gaunt
    b. Straight
    c. Sallow
    d. None of the above

40. The _____ was much more than I expected.

Your _____ will be paid at the end of the day.

    a. Donation
    b. Remuneration
    c. Warning
    d. None of the above

41. High performance cars like that require constant _____.

   a. Maintainance
   b. Maintenace
   c. Maintanance
   d. Maintenance

42. I didn't find it very _____.

   a. Humoros
   b. Humouros
   c. Humorous
   d. Humorus

43. She hasn't been here to my _____.

   a. Knowlege
   b. Knowledge
   c. Knowlegde
   d. Knowlledge

44. I never was very good at _____.

   a. Mathematics
   b. Mathmatics
   c. Matematics
   d. Mathamatics

45. I will look at it when I have some _____ time.

   a. Leisuire
   b. Lesure
   c. Lesure
   d. Leisure

46. Choose the phrase that is not spelled correctly.

a. sufficeint resources
b. collectible coins
c. inconvenient truth
d. fourth revision

47. Choose the phrase that is not spelled correctly.

a. gothic cemetery
b. magicaley disappear
c. broccoli and cheese
d. baked potatoes

48. Choose the phrase that is not spelled correctly.

a. heavy equipmment
b. English grammar
c. weird sounds
d. high intelligence

49. Choose the phrase that is not spelled correctly.

a. foreign accent
b. minature house
c. mischievous elves
d. changeable weather

50. Choose the phrase that is not spelled correctly.

a. turn of the millennium
b. sharp scissors
c. disatrous outcome
d. glass ceiling

Answer Key

Section 1 – Reading

1. A
The correct answer because that fact is stated directly in the passage. The passage explains that Anne taught Helen to hear by allowing her to feel the vibrations in her throat.

2. B
We can infer that Anne is a patient teacher because she did not leave or lose her temper when Helen bit or hit her; she just kept trying to teach Helen. Choice B is incorrect because Anne taught Helen to read and talk. Choice C is incorrect because Anne could hear. She was partially blind, not deaf. Choice D is incorrect because it does not have to do with patience.

3. A
The passage states that it was hard for anyone but Anne to understand Helen when she spoke. Choice A is incorrect because the passage does not mention Helen spoke a foreign language. Choice C is incorrect because there is no mention of how quiet or loud Helen's voice was. Choice D is incorrect because we know from reading the passage that Helen did learn to speak.

4. B
This question tests the reader's summarization skills. The other choices A, B, and C focus on portions of the second paragraph that are too narrow and do not relate to the specific portion of text in question. The complexity of the sentence may mislead students into selecting one of these answers, but rearranging or restating the sentence will lead the reader to the correct answer. In addition, choice A makes an assumption that may or may not be true about the intentions of the company, choice B focuses on one product rather than the idea of the products, and choice C makes an assumption about women that may or may not be true and is not supported by the text.

5. D
This question tests the reader's summarization skills. The question is asking very generally about the message of the passage, and the title, "Ways Characters Communicate in Theater," is one indication of that. The other choices A, B, and C are all directly from the text, and therefore readers may be inclined to select one of them, but are too specific to encapsulate the entirety of the passage and its message.

6. B
The paragraph on soliloquies mentions "To be or not to be," and it is from the context of that paragraph that readers may understand that because "To be or not to be" is a soliloquy, Hamlet will be introspective, or thoughtful, while delivering it. It is true that actors deliver soliloquies alone, and may be "solitary" (choice A), but "thoughtful" (choice B) is more true to the overall idea of the paragraph. Readers may choose C because drama and theater can be used interchangeably and the passage mentions that soliloquies are unique to theater (and therefore drama), but this answer is not specific enough to the paragraph in question. Readers may pick up on the theme of life and death and Hamlet's true intentions and select that he is "hopeless" (choice D), but those themes are not discussed either by this paragraph or passage, as a close textual reading and analysis confirms.

7. C
This question tests the reader's grammatical skills. Choice B seems logical, but parenthesis are actually considered to be a stronger break in a sentence than commas are, and along this line of thinking, actually disrupt the sentence more.

Choices A and D make comparisons between theater and film that are simply not made in the passage, and may or may not be true. This detail does clarify the statement that asides are most unique to theater by adding that it is not completely unique to theater, which may have been why the author didn't chose not to delete it and instead used parentheses to designate the detail's importance (choice C).

8. A
Low blood sugar occurs both in diabetics and healthy adults.

9. B
None of the statements are the author's opinion.

10. A
The author's purpose is the inform.
11. A
The only statement that is not a detail is, "A doctor can diagnosis this medical condition by asking the patient questions and testing."

12. A
This sentence is a recommendation.

13. C
Tips for a good night's sleep is the best alternative title for this article.

14. B
Mental activity is helpful for a good night's sleep is cannot be inferred from this article.

15. A
From the passage, one disadvantage of taking naps is they may keep you awake at night.

16. C
Based on the partial table of contents, you would find information about natural selection in the ecology section on page 110.

17. C
To be infamous means to be remembered for an evil or terrible action. Therefore, the word infamy means to remember a bad or terrible thing. Choice A is incorrect because being famous is not the same as being infamous. Choice B is incorrect because the attack on Pearl Harbor was not good. Choice D is incorrect because Pearl Harbor was not forgotten.

18. C
Each answer choice except choice C contains the name of at least one country that was not part of the AXIS powers.

19. D
It is stated in the passage. Choice A is not correct because there was no indication that Japan would attack San Diego. Choice B is incorrect because the attack on Pearl Harbor was a surprise. Choice C is incorrect because Roosevelt was not planning to attack Japan.

20. C
The passage clearly states that Japan planned a surprise attack. They chose that early time to catch the U.S. military off guard. Choice A is incorrect because the military does not sleep late. Choice B is incorrect because there is no law against bombing countries. Choice D is incorrect because it makes no sense.

21. C
This question tests the reader's vocabulary skills. The uses of the negatives "but" and "less," especially right next to each other, may confuse readers into answering with choices A or D, which list words that are antonyms to "militant." Readers may also be confused by the comparison of healthy people with what is being described as an overly healthy person--both people are good, but the reader may look for which one is "worse" in the comparison, and therefore stray toward the antonym words. The key to understanding the meaning of "militant" is to look at the root of the word; readers can then easily associate it with "military" and gain a sense of what the word signifies: defense (especially considered that the immune system defends the body). Choice C is correct over choice B because "militant" is an adjective, just as the words in choice C are, whereas the words in choice B are nouns.

22. C
This question tests the reader's understanding of function within writing. The other choices are details included surrounding the quoted text, and may therefore confuse the reader. A somewhat contradicts what is said earlier in the paragraph, which is that tests and treatments are improving, and probably doctors are along with them, but the paragraph doesn't actually mention doctors, and the subject of the question is the medicine. Choice B may seem correct to readers who aren't careful to understand that, while the author does mention the large number of people affected,

the author is touching on the realities of living with allergies rather than about the likelihood of curing all allergies. Similarly, while the author does mention the "balance" of the body, which is easily associated with "wholesome," the author is not really making an argument and especially is not making an extreme statement that allergy medicines should be outlawed. Again, because the article's tone is on living with allergies, choice C is an appropriate choice that fits with the title and content of the text.

23. B
This question tests the reader's inference skills. The text does not state who is doing the recommending, but the use of the "patients," as well as the general context of the passage, lends itself to the logical partner, "doctors," choice B. The author does mention the recommendation but doesn't present it as her own (i.e. "I recommend that"), so choice A may be eliminated. It may seem plausible that people with allergies (choice D) may recommend medicines or products to other people with allergies, but the text does not necessarily support this interaction taking place. Choice C may be selected because the EpiPen is specifically mentioned, but the use of the phrase "such as" when it is introduced is not limiting enough to assume the recommendation is coming from its creators.

24. D
This question tests the reader's global understanding of the text. Choice D includes the main topics of the three body paragraphs, and isn't too focused on a specific aspect or quote from the text, as the other questions are, giving a skewed summary of what the author intended. The reader may be drawn to choice B because of the title of the passage and the use of words like "better," but the message of the passage is larger and more general than this.

25. B
Reading the document posted to the Human Resources website is optional.

Mathematics

1. D
75/1500 = 15/300 = 3/60 = 1/20

2. B
Estimate 215 X 65. First start with 200 X 50, which is 10,000, so the answer will be about 10,000. The only choice that is close is 13,500, choice B.

3. B

Day	Number of Absent Students	Number of Present Students	% Attendance
Monday	5	40	88.88%
Tuesday	9	36	80.00%
Wednesday	4	41	91.11%
Thursday	10	35	77.77%
Friday	6	39	86.66%

88.88 + 80.00 + 91.11 + 77.77 + 86.66/5
424.42/5 = 84.88
Round up to 85%.

Percentage attendance will be 85%

4. D
First find a common denominator, 2/3 - 2/5 = 10 - 6 /15 = 4/15

5. C
0.27 + 0.33 = 0.60 and 0.60 = 60/100 = 3/5

6. B
(7 x 7 x 7 x 7 x 7) - (3 x 3 x 3 x 3 x 3) = 16,807 – 243 = 16,564

7. B
2/4 X 3/4 = 6/16, and reduced to the lowest terms = 3/8

8. B
4y + 24 = 3y + 30
4y − 3y = 30 - 24
y = 6

9. B
2/3 x 60 = 40 and 1/5 x 75 = 15, 40 + 15 = 55.

10. A
1/3 X 3/4 = 3/12 = 1/4

11. D
3.13 + 7.87 = 11 and 11 X 5 = 55

12. A
5^6

13. C
Exponential form is 9^3 and standard from is 729

14. B
$(4)(3)^3$ = (4)(27) = 108

15. B
0.524/ 10 x 10 x 10 = 0.524/1000 = 0.000524

16. C
3x - 27 = 0
3x = 27
x = 9

17. C
First convert to decimal 7/11 = .63 and 5/7 = .714
2/3, choice C (.667) is the only choice between the two given numbers.

18. B
0.25 + 0.65 = 0.9 = 9/10

19. C
 389 + 454 = 843

20. C
9,177 + 7,204 = 16,381

21. D
2,199 + 5,832 = 8,031

22. B
8,390 - 5,239 = 3,151

23. A
643 - 587 = 56

24. C
3,406 - 2,767 = 639

25. B
149 × 7 = 1043

Applied Mathematics

1. D
The formula for volume of a shape is L x W x H = 20 x 20 x 20 = 8,000 cm³

2. D
Let old salary = X, therefore $150 = x + 0.30x, 150 = 1x + 0.30x, 150 = 1.30x, x = 150/1.30 = 115.4

3. C
Cash = 51,300 + $75600 = $126,900. Building after one year = 80500 X 1.1 = $88550. Machinery after one year = 125000 X 0.8 = $100000. Total asset value = $315,450.

4.   C
If there are 5 friends and each drink costs $1.89, we can round up to $2 per drink and estimate the total cost at, 5 X $2 = $10.

The actual cost is 5 X $1.89 = $9.45.

5. A
At 100% efficiency 1 machine produces 1450/10 = 145 m of cloth.

Practice Test Questions 1 217

At 95% efficiency, 4 machines produce (4 * 145 * 95)/100 = 551 m of cloth.

At 90% efficiency, 6 machines produce (6 * 145 * 90)/100 = 783 m of cloth.

Total cloth produced by all 10 machines = 551 + 783 = 1334 m

Since the information provided and the question are based on 8 hours, we did not need to use time to reach the answer.

6. A
The correct equation is X + 0.005xy.

7. A
The graph shows oil consumption peaked in 2011.

8. D
To find the total turnout in all three polling stations, we need to proportion the number of voters to the number of all registered voters.

Total number of voters = 945 + 860 + 1210 = 3015

Total number of registered voters = 1270 + 1050 + 1440 = 3760

Percentage turnout in all three polling stations = 3015•100/3760 = 80.19%

Check the answer, ound 80.19 to the nearest whole number: 80%

9. B
Total expenses = 5284.34 + $8,384.76 + $2,920.00 = 16589.10

Profit = revenue less expenses

$19,304.56 - $16,589.10 = $2,715.46

10. D
The formula for area is S (squared), and if the perimeter is 100, each side will be 25, the the area is 25 squared.

11. B
40% of 8.50 = 8.5 X .4 = $3.40. Including tips, $3.40 + 1.30 = $4.70

12. D
Taking Mr. Jones's total to calculate the price of an adult ticket, 38.5/7 = 5.5. Mr. Jones bought 9 adult tickets for a cost of 9 X 5.5 = $49.50.

Total cost was 67, so to calculate the cost of children's ticket, 67 - 49.5 = 17.5. 17.5/5 = $3.50

13. C
Equilateral triangle with 9 cm. sides
Perimeter = 9 + 9 + 9 = 27 cm.

14. D
Perimeter of triangle ABC is asked.
Perimeter of a triangle = sum of the three sides.

Here, Perimeter of $\triangle ABC$ = |AC| + |CB| + |AB|.

Since the triangle is located in the middle of two adjacent and identical rectangles, we find the side lengths using these rectangles:

|AB| = 6 + 6 = 12 cm

|CB| = 8.5 cm

|AC| = |CB| = 8.5 cm

Perimeter = |AC| + |CB| + |AB| = 8.5 + 8.5 + 12 = 29 cm

15. B
She spent 15% - 100% - 15% = 85%

16. D
Formula for volume of a shape is L x W x H = 10 x 8 x 10 = 800 cm^3

17. B
This is a compound interest problem. Calculate the interest earned in the first year and then use that total for the second year calculation.

In the first year, 5000 X .04 = 200
In the second year, 5200 X .04 = 208
Total at the end of the second year = $5408

18. B
The distribution is at three different rates and amounts:

$6.4 per 20 kilograms to 15 shops ... 20 * 15 = 300 kilograms distributed

$3.4 per 10 kilograms to 12 shops ... 10 * 12 = 120 kilograms distributed

550 - (300 + 120) = 550 - 420 = 130 kilograms left. This amount is distributed by 5 kilogram portions. So, this means that there are 130/5 = 26 shops.

$1.8 per 130 kilograms.

We need to find the amount he earned overall these distributions.

$6.4 per 20 kilograms : 6.4 * 15 = $96 for 300 kilograms

$3.4 per 10 kilograms : 3.4 * 12 = $40.8 for 120 kilograms

$1.8 per 5 kilograms : 1.8 * 26 = $46.8 for 130 kilograms

So, he earned 96 + 40.8 + 46.8 = $ 183.6

The total distribution cost is given as $10

The profit is found by: Money earned - money spent ... It is important to remember that he bought 550 kilograms of potatoes for $165 at the beginning:

Profit = 183.6 - 10 - 165 = $8.6

19. D
The distance covered by the car = 60 X 3.5 = 210 km. Time required by the motorbike = 210/40 = 5.25 hr.

20. D
The number is 51.738. The last digit is greater than 5, so it is removed and 1 is added to the next number to the left. Answer = 51.74.

21. C
The ratio between gold, silver and bronze coins is 2:6:12. Bring to the lowest terms by dividing each element in the original ratio by 2 gives 1:3:6.

22. B
The line is pointing towards numbers less than 1. The equation is therefore, X < 1.

23. A
The line is pointing towards numbers greater than 2. The equation is therefore, X < 2.

24. C
The decimal point moves 9 spaces right to be placed after 7, which is the first non-zero number. Thus 7.892×10^9

25. D
Each time the * and + alternate, either singly or doubles.

English

1. D
Use an exclamation mark after an imperative sentence if the command is urgent and forceful.

2. A
A comma is used before the conjunction to separate two independent clauses in a compound sentence.

3. C
A semicolon is also used to join two clauses that present a direct contrast. In this question, the sentence has two extremes in a similar situation. Notice that even when the two clauses present a contrast, the subjects of the two clauses are similar.

4. C
A semi colon may also be used to prevent confusion. The other obvious choice is this sentence would be a comma, but it isn't a choice.

5. A
A comma is used to separate three or more words, phrases or clauses in a series.

6. C
The semicolon links independent clauses.

7. A
The semicolon links independent clauses with a conjunction (However).

8. B
The semicolon links independent clauses.

9. D
A colon informs the reader that what follows the mark proves, explains, or lists elements of what preceded the mark.

10. A
A colon informs the reader that what follows the mark proves, explains, or lists elements of what preceded the mark.

11. A
Choice A is the only choice that includes quotation marks around the quoted speech and a question mark.

12. A
In choice A, "city" is capitalized because it is used in the phrase, "City of Miami." "Florida" in this sentence is also correctly capitalized. Choice B does not capitalize "Florida." Choice C omits an apostrophe in "California's best beaches." Choice D does not capitalize "Brooklyn."

13. B
Choice A has incorrect capitalization of "Wall Street Journal." The names of publications are capitalized. Choice C

incorrect capitalizes "Weekend Newspaper." Choice D incorrectly capitalizes "USA Today."

14. D
Choice A uses commas incorrectly. Choice B uses both commas and capitalization incorrectly, and choice D uses a dash where it is not required.

15. A
Choice A correctly capitalizes the singers name, includes the name of the song in quotes, as well as capitalizes "Grammys." Choice B does not include the name of the song in quotes. Choice C incorrectly uses dashes, and choice D incorrectly uses quotation marks.

16. C
17. A
18. B
19. D
20. A
21. C
22. C
23. C
24. D
25. B
26. D
The sentence is correct. The other choices add an additional and unnecessary comma.

27. A
"Equipt" is incorrect - the correct form is "equipped with."

28. D
The phrase, "function of some insects" is singular, so "is" is correct.

29. C
The correct usage for comparing two things is "difference between."

30. A
Choice A uses the contraction "it's" correctly.

Vocabulary

31. C
Veterinarian: a person qualified to treat diseased or injured animals.

32. A
Immune: resistant to a particular virus or toxin.

33. D
Pesticide: a substance used for destroying insects or other organisms harmful to cultivated plants or to animals.

34. A
Famine: extreme scarcity of food.

35. B
Hormones: a regulatory substance produced in an organism and transported in tissue fluids such as blood or sap to stimulate specific cells or tissues into action.

36. A
Maverick: Showing independence in thoughts or actions.

37. C
Pandemonium: wild and noisy disorder or confusion; uproar.

38. B
Dissipate: disperse or scatter.

39. A
Gaunt: lean and haggard, esp. because of suffering, hunger, or age.

40. B
Remuneration: A payment for work done; wages, salary.

Spelling

41. D
Maintenance is the correct spelling.

42. C
Humorous is the correct spelling.

43. B
Knowledge is the correct spelling.

44. A
Mathematics is the correct spelling.

45. D
Leisure is the correct spelling.

46. A
Sufficeint is incorrect. The correct spelling is sufficient.

47. B
Magicaley is incorrect. The correct spelling is magically.

48. A
Equipmment is incorrect. The correct spelling is equipment.

49. B
Minature is incorrect. The correct spelling is miniature.

50. C
Disatrous is incorrect. The correct spelling is disastrous.

Practice Test Questions Set 2

The practice test portion presents questions that are representative of the type of question you should expect to find on the TABE®. However, they are not intended to match exactly what is on the TABE®.

For the best results, take this Practice Test as if it were the real exam. Set aside time when you will not be disturbed, and a location that is quiet and free of distractions. Read the instructions carefully, read each question carefully, and answer to the best of your ability.

Use the bubble answer sheets provided. When you have completed the Practice Test, check your answer against the Answer Key and read the explanation provided.

Reading

	A	B	C	D	E		A	B	C	D	E
1	○	○	○	○	○	21	○	○	○	○	○
2	○	○	○	○	○	22	○	○	○	○	○
3	○	○	○	○	○	23	○	○	○	○	○
4	○	○	○	○	○	24	○	○	○	○	○
5	○	○	○	○	○	25	○	○	○	○	○
6	○	○	○	○	○						
7	○	○	○	○	○						
8	○	○	○	○	○						
9	○	○	○	○	○						
10	○	○	○	○	○						
11	○	○	○	○	○						
12	○	○	○	○	○						
13	○	○	○	○	○						
14	○	○	○	○	○						
15	○	○	○	○	○						
16	○	○	○	○	○						
17	○	○	○	○	○						
18	○	○	○	○	○						
19	○	○	○	○	○						
20	○	○	○	○	○						

Computational Mathematics

	A	B	C	D	E		A	B	C	D	E
1	○	○	○	○	○	21	○	○	○	○	○
2	○	○	○	○	○	22	○	○	○	○	○
3	○	○	○	○	○	23	○	○	○	○	○
4	○	○	○	○	○	24	○	○	○	○	○
5	○	○	○	○	○	25	○	○	○	○	○
6	○	○	○	○	○						
7	○	○	○	○	○						
8	○	○	○	○	○						
9	○	○	○	○	○						
10	○	○	○	○	○						
11	○	○	○	○	○						
12	○	○	○	○	○						
13	○	○	○	○	○						
14	○	○	○	○	○						
15	○	○	○	○	○						
16	○	○	○	○	○						
17	○	○	○	○	○						
18	○	○	○	○	○						
19	○	○	○	○	○						
20	○	○	○	○	○						

Applied Mathematics

	A	B	C	D	E			A	B	C	D	E
1	○	○	○	○	○		21	○	○	○	○	○
2	○	○	○	○	○		22	○	○	○	○	○
3	○	○	○	○	○		23	○	○	○	○	○
4	○	○	○	○	○		24	○	○	○	○	○
5	○	○	○	○	○		25	○	○	○	○	○
6	○	○	○	○	○							
7	○	○	○	○	○							
8	○	○	○	○	○							
9	○	○	○	○	○							
10	○	○	○	○	○							
11	○	○	○	○	○							
12	○	○	○	○	○							
13	○	○	○	○	○							
14	○	○	○	○	○							
15	○	○	○	○	○							
16	○	○	○	○	○							
17	○	○	○	○	○							
18	○	○	○	○	○							
19	○	○	○	○	○							
20	○	○	○	○	○							

Language

	A	B	C	D	E		A	B	C	D	E
1	○	○	○	○	○	21	○	○	○	○	○
2	○	○	○	○	○	22	○	○	○	○	○
3	○	○	○	○	○	23	○	○	○	○	○
4	○	○	○	○	○	24	○	○	○	○	○
5	○	○	○	○	○	25	○	○	○	○	○
6	○	○	○	○	○	26	○	○	○	○	○
7	○	○	○	○	○	27	○	○	○	○	○
8	○	○	○	○	○	28	○	○	○	○	○
9	○	○	○	○	○	29	○	○	○	○	○
10	○	○	○	○	○	30	○	○	○	○	○
11	○	○	○	○	○	31	○	○	○	○	○
12	○	○	○	○	○	32	○	○	○	○	○
13	○	○	○	○	○	33	○	○	○	○	○
14	○	○	○	○	○	34	○	○	○	○	○
15	○	○	○	○	○	35	○	○	○	○	○
16	○	○	○	○	○	36	○	○	○	○	○
17	○	○	○	○	○	37	○	○	○	○	○
18	○	○	○	○	○	38	○	○	○	○	○
19	○	○	○	○	○	39	○	○	○	○	○
20	○	○	○	○	○	40	○	○	○	○	○

Reading and Language Arts

Questions 1 - 4 refer to the following passage.

Passage 1 - The Crusades

In 1095 Pope Urban II proclaimed the First Crusade with the intent and stated goal to restore Christian access to holy places in and around Jerusalem. Over the next 200 years there were 6 major crusades and numerous minor crusades in the fight for control of the "Holy Land." Historians are divided on the real purpose of the Crusades, some believing that it was part of a purely defensive war against Islamic conquest; some see them as part of a long-running conflict at the frontiers of Europe; and others see them as confident, aggressive, papal-led expansion attempts by Western Christendom. The impact of the crusades was profound, and judgment of the Crusaders ranges from laudatory to highly critical. However, all agree that the Crusades and wars waged during those crusades were brutal and often bloody. Several hundred thousand Roman Catholic Christians joined the Crusades, they were Christians from all over Europe.

Europe at the time was under the Feudal System, so while the Crusaders made vows to the Church they also were beholden to their Feudal Lords. This led to the Crusaders not only fighting the Saracen, the commonly used word for Muslim at the time, but also each other for power and economic gain in the Holy Land. This infighting between the Crusaders is why many historians hold the view that the Crusades were simply a front for Europe to invade the Holy Land for economic gain in the name of the Church. Another factor contributing to this theory is that while the army of crusaders marched towards Jerusalem they pillaged the land as they went. The church and feudal Lords vowing to return the land to its original beauty, and inhabitants, this rarely happened though as the Lords often kept the land for themselves. A full 800 years after the Crusades, Pope John Paul II expressed his sorrow for the massacre of innocent people and the lasting damage the Medieval church caused in that area of the World.

Practice Test Questions 2

1. What is the tone of this article?

   a. Subjective
   b. Objective
   c. Persuasive
   d. None of the Above

2. What can all historians agree on concerning the Crusades?

   a. It achieved great things
   b. It stabilized the Holy Land
   c. It was bloody and brutal
   d. It helped defend Europe from the Byzantine Empire

3. What impact did the feudal system have on the Crusades?

   a. It unified the Crusaders
   b. It helped gather volunteers
   c. It had no effect on the Crusades
   d. It led to infighting, causing more damage than good

4. What does Saracen mean?

   a. Muslim
   b. Christian
   c. Knight
   d. Holy Land

Questions 5 - 8 refer to the following passage.

ABC Electric Warranty

ABC Electric Company warrants that its products are free from defects in material and workmanship. Subject to the conditions and limitations set forth below, ABC Electric will, at its option, either repair or replace any part of its products that prove defective due to improper workmanship or materials.

This limited warranty does not cover any damage to the product from improper installation, accident, abuse, misuse, natural disaster, insufficient or excessive electrical supply, abnormal mechanical or environmental conditions, or any unauthorized disassembly, repair, or modification.

This limited warranty also does not apply to any product on which the original identification information has been altered, or removed, has not been handled or packaged correctly, or has been sold as second-hand.

This limited warranty covers only repair, replacement, refund or credit for defective ABC Electric products, as provided above.

5. I tried to repair my ABC Electric blender, but could not, so can I get it repaired under this warranty?

    a. Yes, the warranty still covers the blender

    b. No, the warranty does not cover the blender

    c. Uncertain. ABC Electric may or may not cover repairs under this warranty

6. My ABC Electric fan is not working. Will ABC Electric provide a new one or repair this one?

    a. ABC Electric will repair my fan

    b. ABC Electric will replace my fan

    c. ABC Electric could either replace or repair my fan can request either a replacement or a repair.

7. My stove was damaged in a flood. Does this warranty cover my stove?

    a. Yes, it is covered.

    b. No, it is not covered.

    c. It may or may not be covered.

    d. ABC Electric will decide if it is covered

8. Which of the following is an example of improper workmanship?

    a. Missing parts

    b. Defective parts

    c. Scratches on the front

    d. None of the above

Questions 9 – 12 refer to the following passage.

Passage 2 - Women and Advertising

Only in the last few generations have media messages been so widespread and so readily seen, heard, and read by so many people. Advertising is an important part of both selling and buying anything from soap to cereal to jeans. For whatever reason, more consumers are women than are men. Media message are subtle but powerful, and more attention has been paid latcly to how these message affect women. Of all the products that women buy, makeup, clothes, and other stylistic or cosmetic products are among the most popular. This means that companies focus their advertising on women, promising them that their product will make her feel, look, or smell better than the next company's product will. This competition has resulted in advertising that is more and more ideal and less and less possible for everyday women. However, because women do look to these ideals and the products they represent as how they can potentially become, many women have developed unhealthy attitudes about themselves when they have failed to become those ideals.

In recent years, more companies have tried to change advertisements to be healthier for women. This includes featuring models of more sizes and addressing a huge outcry against unfair tools such as airbrushing and photo editing. There is debate about what the right balance between real and ideal is, because fashion is also considered art and some changes are made to purposefully elevate fashionable products and signify that they are creative, innovative, and the work of individual people. Artists want their freedom protected as much as women do, and advertising agencies are often caught in the middle.

Some claim that the companies who make these changes are not doing enough. Many people worry that there are still not enough models of different sizes and different ethnicities. Some people claim that companies use this healthier type of advertisement not for the good of women, but because they would like to sell products to the women who are looking for these kinds of messages. This is also a hard balance to find: companies do need to make money, and women do need to feel respected.

While the focus of this change has been on women, advertising can also affect men, and this change will hopefully be a lesson on media for all consumers.

9. The second paragraph states that advertising focuses on women

      a. to shape what the ideal should be

      b. because women buy makeup

      c. because women are easily persuaded

      d. because of the types of products that women buy

10. According to the passage, fashion artists and female consumers are at odds because

    a. there is a debate going on and disagreement drives people apart

    b. both of them are trying to protect their freedom to do something

    c. artists want to elevate their products above the reach of women

    d. women are creative, innovative, individual people

11. The author uses the phrase "for whatever reason" in this passage to

    a. keep the focus of the paragraph on media messages and not on the differences between men and women

    b. show that the reason for this is unimportant

    c. argue that it is stupid that more women are consumers than men

    d. show that he or she is tired of talking about why media messages are important

12. This passage suggests that

    a. advertising companies are still working on making their messages better

    b. all advertising companies seek to be more approachable for women

    c. women are only buying from companies that respect them

    d. artists could stop producing fashionable products if they feel bullied

Questions 13 - 16 refer to the following passage.

FDR, the Treaty of Versailles, and the Fourteen Points

At the conclusion of World War I, those who had won the war and those who were forced to admit defeat welcomed the end of the war and expected that a peace treaty would be signed. The American president, Franklin D. Roosevelt, played an important part in proposing what the agreements should be and did so through his Fourteen Points.
World War I had begun in 1914 when an Austrian archduke was assassinated, leading to a domino effect that pulled the world's most powerful countries into war on a large scale. The war catalyzed the creation and use of deadly weapons that had not previously existed, resulting in a great loss of soldiers on both sides of the fighting. More than 9 million soldiers were killed.

The United States agreed to enter the war right before it ended, and many believed that its decision to become finally involved brought on the end of the war. FDR made it very clear that the U.S. was entering the war for moral reasons and had an agenda focused on world peace. The Fourteen Points were individual goals and ideas (focused on peace, free trade, open communication, and self reliance) that FDR wanted the power nations to strive for now that the war had concluded. He was optimistic and had many ideas about what could be accomplished through and during the post-war peace. However, FDR's fourteen points were poorly received when he presented them to the leaders of other world powers, many of whom wanted only to help their own countries and to punish the Germans for fueling the war, and they fell by the wayside. World War II was imminent, for Germany lost everything.

Some historians believe that the other leaders who participated in the Treaty of Versailles weren't receptive to the Fourteen Points because World War I was fought almost entirely on European soil, and the United States lost much less than did the other powers. FDR was in a unique position to determine the fate of the war, but doing it on his own terms did not help accomplish his goals. This is only one historical example of how the United State has tried to use its power as an important country, but found itself limited because of geological or ideological factors.

13. The main idea of this passage is that

   a. World War I was unfair because no fighting took place in America

   b. World War II happened because of the Treaty of Versailles

   c. the power the United States has to help other countries also prevents it from helping other countries

   d. Franklin D. Roosevelt was one of the United States' smartest presidents

14. According to the second paragraph, World War I started because

   a. an archduke was assassinated

   b. weapons that were more deadly had been developed

   c. a domino effect of allies agreeing to help each other

   d. the world's most powerful countries were large

15. The author includes the detail that 9 million soldiers were killed

   a. to demonstrate why European leaders were hesitant to accept peace

   b. to show the reader the dangers of deadly weapons

   c. to make the reader think about which countries lost the most soldiers

   d. to demonstrate why World War II was imminent

16. According to this passage, the word catalyzed means

a. analyzed
b. sped up
c. invented
d. funded

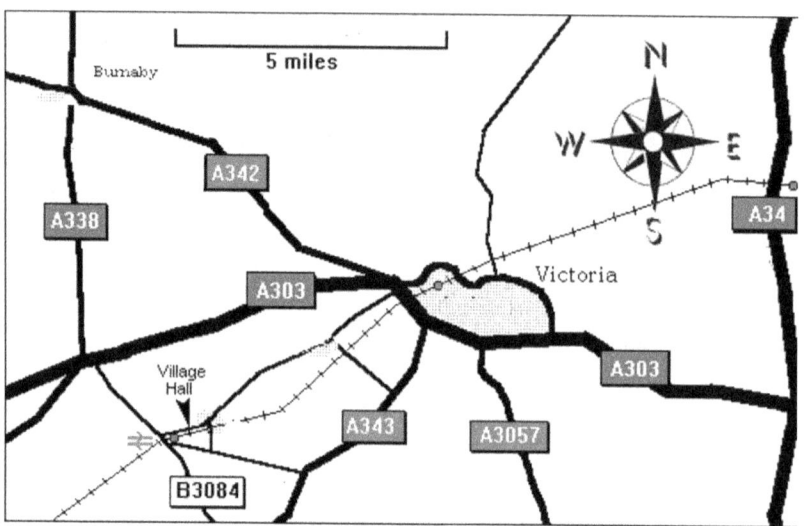

17. Approximately how far is Victoria to Burnaby?

a. About 10 miles
b. About 5 miles
c. About 15 miles
d. About 20 miles

18. How is the Village Hall from Victoria?

a. About 10 miles
b. About 5 miles
c. About 15 miles
d. About 20 miles

Questions 19 - 22 refer to the following passage.

Chocolate Chip Cookies

3/4 cup sugar
3/4 cup packed brown sugar
1 cup butter, softened
2 large eggs, beaten
1 teaspoon vanilla extract
2 1/4 cups all-purpose flour
1 teaspoon baking soda
3/4 teaspoon salt
2 cups semisweet chocolate chips
If desired, 1 cup chopped pecans, or chopped walnuts.
Preheat oven to 375 degrees.

Mix sugar, brown sugar, butter, vanilla and eggs in a large bowl. Stir in flour, baking soda, and salt. The dough will be very stiff.

Stir in chocolate chips by hand with a sturdy wooden spoon. Add the pecans, or other nuts, if desired. Stir until the chocolate chips and nuts are evenly dispersed.

Drop dough by rounded tablespoonfuls 2 inches apart onto a cookie sheet.

Bake 8 to 10 minutes or until light brown. Cookies may look underdone, but they will finish cooking after you take them out of the oven.

19. What is the correct order for adding these ingredients?

    a. Brown sugar, baking soda, chocolate chips
    b. Baking soda, brown sugar, chocolate chips
    c. Chocolate chips, baking soda, brown sugar
    d. Baking soda, chocolate chips, brown sugar

20. What does sturdy mean?

  a. Long
  b. Strong
  c. Short
  d. Wide

21. What does disperse mean?

  a. Scatter
  b. To form a ball
  c. To stir
  d. To beat

22. When can you stop stirring the nuts?

  a. When the cookies are cooked.
  b. When the nuts are evenly distributed.
  c. When the nuts are added.
  d. After the chocolate chips are added.

Questions 23 - 26 refer to the following passage.

Passage 5 - Frankenstein

Great God! What a scene has just taken place! I am yet dizzy with the remembrance of it. I hardly know whether I shall have the power to detail it; yet the tale which I have recorded would be incomplete without this final and wonderful catastrophe. I entered the cabin where lay the remains of my ill-fated and admirable friend. Over him hung a form which I cannot find words to describe—gigantic in stature, yet uncouth and distorted in its proportions. As he hung over the coffin, his face was concealed by long locks of ragged hair; but one vast hand was extended, in color and apparent texture like that of a mummy. When he heard the sound of my approach, he ceased to utter exclamations of grief and horror and sprung towards the window. Never did I behold a vision so horrible as his face, of such loathsome yet appalling hideousness. I shut my eyes involuntarily and endeavored to recollect what were my duties with regard to this destroyer. I called on him to stay.

He paused, looking on me with wonder, and again turning towards the lifeless form of his creator, he seemed to forget my presence, and every feature and gesture seemed instigated by the wildest rage of some uncontrollable passion.

"That is also my victim!" he exclaimed. "In his murder my crimes are consummated; the miserable series of my being is wound to its close! Oh, Frankenstein! Generous and self-devoted being! What does it avail that I now ask thee to pardon me? I, who irretrievably destroyed thee by destroying all thou lovedst. Alas! He is cold, he cannot answer me."

His voice seemed suffocated, and my first impulses, which had suggested to me the duty of obeying the dying request of my friend in destroying his enemy, were now suspended by a mixture of curiosity and compassion. I approached this tremendous being; I dared not again raise my eyes to his face, there was something so scaring and unearthly in his ugliness. I attempted to speak, but the words died away on my lips. The monster continued to utter wild and incoherent self-reproaches. At length I gathered resolution to address him in a pause of the tempest of his passion.

"Your repentance," I said, "is now superfluous. If you had listened to the voice of conscience and heeded the stings of remorse before you had urged your diabolical vengeance to this extremity, Frankenstein would yet have lived." [7]

23. Who is the "ill-fated and admirable friend" who is lying in the coffin?

    a. Frankenstein's monster

    b. Frankenstein

    c. Mary Shelley

    d. Unknown

24. Why is the speaker 'suspended" from following through on his duty to destroy the monster?

    a. The way the monster looks

    b. The monster's remorse

    c. Curiosity and compassion

    d. Fear the monster might kill him too

25. How does Frankenstein's monster destroy Frankenstein?

    a. By killing Frankenstein

    b. By letting himself be the monster everyone sees him as

    c. By destroying everything Frankenstein loved

    d. All of the above

Computational Mathematics

1. 8974 – 8256 =

    a. 715

    b. 716

    c. 718

    d. 715

2. 4404 / 8 =

    a. 550.5

    b. 550

    c. 505

    d. 555

3. 274 * 139 =

    a. 38006
    b. 38860
    c. 38060
    d. 38086

4. 3567 + 99 =

    a. 3066
    b. 3666
    c. 3606
    d. 4666

5. Translate the following into an equation:

2 plus a number divided by 7.

    a. (2 + X)/7
    b. (7 + X)/2
    c. (2 + 7)/X
    d. 2/(7 + X)

6. 60 is 75% of x. Solve for x.

    a. 80
    b. 90
    c. 75
    d. 70

7. Express 71/1000 as a decimal.

    a. .71
    b. .0071
    c. .071
    d. 7.1

8. .33 × .59 =

    a. .1947
    b. 1.95
    c. .0197
    d. .1817

9. 7x – 9 = 47. Solve for x.

    a. 8
    b. 7
    c. 9
    d. 6

10. What number is in the ten thousandths place in 1.7389

    a. 1
    b. 8
    c. 9
    d. 3

11. .87 - .48 =

    a. .39
    b. .49
    c. .41
    d. .37

12. Which is the equivalent decimal number for forty nine thousandths?

    a. .49
    b. .0049
    c. .049
    d. 4.9

13. Which of the following is not a fraction equivalent to 3/4?

   a. 6/8
   b. 9/12
   c. 12/18
   d. 21/28

14. Which one of the following is greater than a third?

   a. 84/231
   b. 6/35
   c. 3/22
   d. b and c

15. Which of the following numbers is the greatest?

   a. 1
   b. $\sqrt{2}$
   c. 3/2
   d. 4/3

16. 2b + 9b − 5b = 0

   a. 3b
   b. 6b
   c. 4b
   d. 8b

17. 4.7 + .9 + .01 =

   a. 5.5
   b. 6.51
   c. 5.61
   d. 5.7

18. 60% of x is 12. Solve for x.

    a. 18
    b. 15
    c. 25
    d. 20

19. .84 ÷ .7 =

    a. .12
    b. 12
    c. .012
    d. 1.2

20. 4120 − 3216 =

    a. 903
    b. 804
    c. 904
    d. 1904

21. 2417 + 1004 =

    a. 3401
    b. 4321
    c. 3402
    d. 3421

22. Simplify 0.12 + 1 2/5 − 1 3/5

    a. 1 1/25
    b. -2/25
    c. 1 2/5
    d. 2 3/5

23. What is the difference between 700,653 and 70,099?

  a. 4607854
  b. 5460
  c. 700765
  d. 630,554

24. Simplify 0.25 + 1/3 + 2/3

  a. 1 1/4
  b. 2 1/4
  c. 1 1/3
  d. 2 1/4

25. Add 10% of 300 to 50% of 20

  a. 50
  b. 40
  c. 60
  d. 45

Applied Mathematics

1. If a train travels at 72 kilometers per hour, how far will it travel in 12 seconds?

  a. 200m
  b. 220m
  c. 240m
  d. 260m

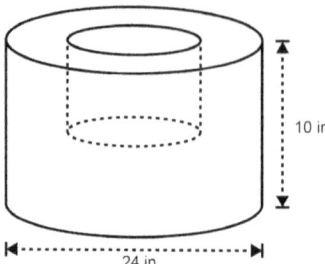

Note: Figure not drawn to scale

2. What is the volume of the above solid made by a hollow cylinder that is half the size (in all dimensions) of the larger cylinder?

    a. 1440 π in³
    b. 1260 π in³
    c. 1040 π in³
    d. 960 π in³

3. Tony bought 15 dozen eggs for $80. 16 eggs were broken during loading and unloading. He sold the remaining eggs for $0.54 each. What will be his percent profit?

    a. 11%
    b. 10%
    c. 13%
    d. 12%

4. In a class of 83 students, 72 are present. What percent of students are absent?

    a. 12%
    b. 13%
    c. 14%
    d. 15%

5. A student deposits $200 in a savings account hoping to buy a bicycle worth $245. If the bank offers a 15% interest rate, how long will she have to wait?

   a. 1½ years
   b. 2 ½ years
   c. 2 years
   d. 1 year

6. A man earns $600 as interest after 2 years of depositing a certain amount in a local bank. If the interest rate was 3%, how much was the original amount deposited?

   a. $3,600
   b. $100,000
   c. $10,000
   d. $1,000

Consider the following graph.

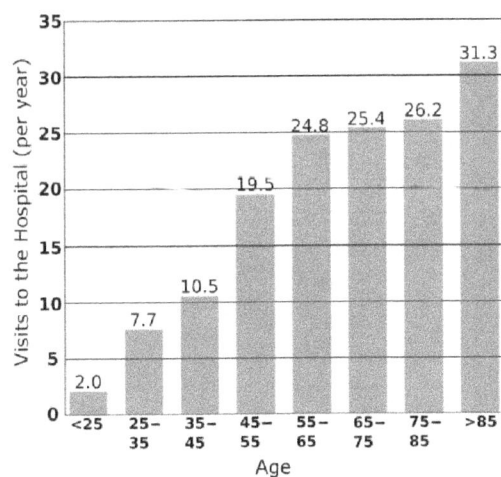

7. How many hospital visits per year does a person aged 85 or older make?

    a. 26.2

    b. 31.3

    c. More than 31.3

    d. A decision cannot be made from this graph.

8. Based on this graph, how many visits per year do you expect a person that is 95 or older to make?

    a. More than 31.3

    b. Less than 31.3

    c. 31.3

    d. A decision cannot be made from this graph.

9. How much water can be stored in a cylindrical container 5 meters in diameter and 12 meters high?

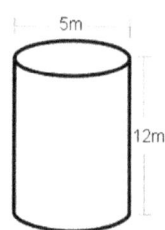

Note: Figure not drawn to scale

    a. 235.65 m³

    b. 223.65 m³

    c. 240.65 m³

    d. 252.65 m³

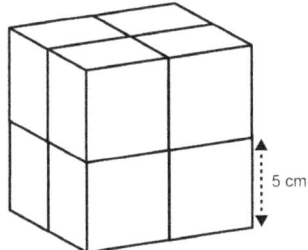

5 cm

Note: Figure not drawn to scale

10. Assuming the figure has cubes, what is the volume of the figure above?

    a. 125 cm³
    b. 875 cm³
    c. 1000 cm³
    d. 500 cm³

11. Choose the expression the figure represents.

    a. X > 2
    b. X ≥ 2
    c. X < 2
    d. X ≤ 2

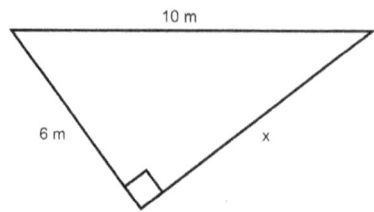

12. What is the length of the missing side in the triangle above?

    a. 6
    b. 4
    c. 8
    d. 5

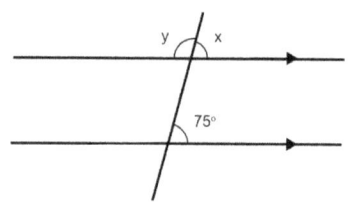

13. What is the value of the angle y?

    a. 25°
    b. 15°
    c. 30°
    d. 105°

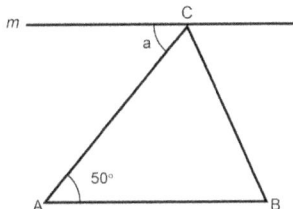

14. If the line *m* is parallel to the side AB of △ABC, what is angle *a*?

    a. 130°
    b. 25°
    c. 65°
    d. 50°

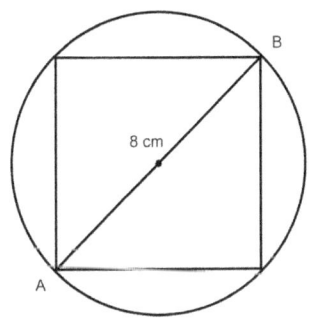

Note: Figure not drawn to scale

15. What is area of the circle?

    a. 4 π cm²
    b. 12 π cm²
    c. 10 π cm²
    d. 16 π cm²

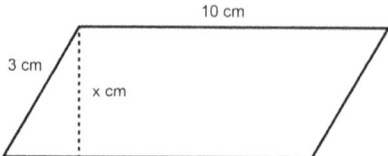

16. What is the perimeter of the parallelogram above?

    a. 12 cm
    b. 26 cm
    c. 13 cm
    d. (13+x) cm

17. Express 87% as a decimal.

    a. .087
    b. 8.7
    c. .87
    d. 87

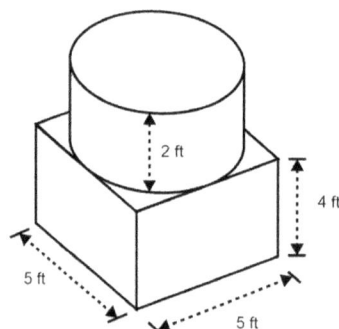

Note: Figure not drawn to scale

18. What is the approximate total volume of the above solid?

    a. 120 ft³

    b. 100 ft³

    c. 140 ft³

    d. 160 ft³

19. Susan wants to buy a leather jacket that costs $545.00 and is on sale for 10% off. What is the approximate cost?

    a. $525

    b. $450

    c. $475

    d. $500

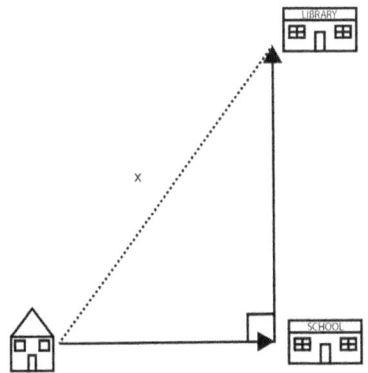

Note: Figure not drawn to scale

20. Every day starting from his home Peter travels due east 3 kilometers to the school. After school he travels due north 4 kilometers to the library. What is the distance between Peter's home and the library?

    a. 15 km

    b. 10 km

    c. 5 km

    d. 12 ½ km

21. If Tim deposits $5,500 in a savings account that offers a 5% interest, what will be the total amount in his savings account after 3 years?

    a. $6,225
    b. $6,0325
    c. $325
    d. $6,325

22. The cost of waterproofing canvas is .50 per square yard. What is the total cost for waterproofing a canvas truck cover that is 15' x 24'?

    a. $18.00
    b. $6.67
    c. $180.00
    d. $20.00

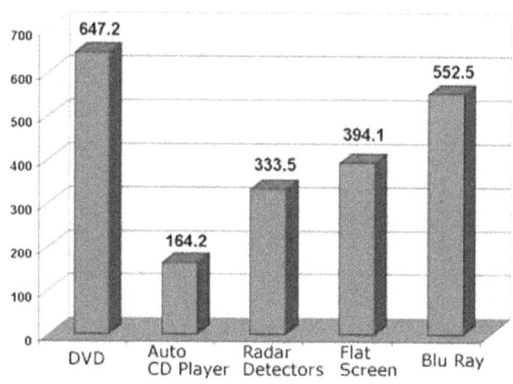

23. Consider the graph above. What is the third best-selling product?

    a. Radar Detectors
    b. Flat Screen TV
    c. Blu Ray
    d. Auto CD Players

24. Which two products are the closest in the number of sales?

    a. Blu Ray and Flat Screen TV
    b. Flat Screen TV and Radar Detectors
    c. Radar Detectors and Auto CD Players
    d. DVD players and Blu Ray

25. A small business owner deposits $6000 in a savings account at a local bank. After 2 years, at 3% interest rate, what will be the interest earned?

    a. $6360
    b. $360
    c. $240
    d. $460

Language

Directions: Fill in the blank with the correct punctuation.

1. The recipe requires the following ingredients _____ flour, sugar, eggs, baking powder and vanilla.

    a. ,
    b. :
    c. ;
    d. .

2. Lindsay said _____ "It's a beautiful day."

    a. ,
    b. :
    c. ;
    d. .

3. Dear Ms. Smith___

    a. :
    b. ,
    c. .
    d. !

4. Her sister___s bag was full of useless items

    a. " "
    b. '
    c. ,
    d. –

5. Actors try to empathize with ___ to share the feelings of ___ the characters they portray.

    a. ( )
    b. { }
    c. [ ]
    d. " "

6. Choose the sentence below with the correct punctuation.

    a. Puzzled — Joe said, "You aren't going to pay me until ?"
    b. Puzzled, Joe said, "You aren't going to pay me until ?"
    c. Puzzled, Joe said, "You aren't going to pay me until —?"
    d. Puzzled, Joe said, "You aren't going to pay me until, ?"

7. Choose the sentence below with the correct punctuation.

a. His employment wasn't consecutive, from 1999 to 2001 and 2002 – 2004.

b. His employment wasn't consecutive, from 1999 – 2001 and 2002 – 2004.

c. His employment wasn't consecutive, from 1999 _ 2001   and 2002_ 2004.

d. His employment wasn't consecutive, from 1999, 2001 and 2002, 2004.

8. Choose the sentence below with the correct punctuation.

a. Sandy asked for a one/third reduction on the cost of her damaged bag.

b. Sandy asked for a one, third reduction on the cost of her damaged bag.

c. Sandy asked for a one-third reduction on the cost of her damaged bag.

d. None of the Above.

9. Choose the sentence below with the correct punctuation.

a. Three minutes, two minutes, one minute

b. Three minutes ... two minutes ... one minutes

c. Three minutes - two minutes - one minutes

d. None of the Above.

10. Choose the sentence below with the correct punctuation.

    a. Ms. Hermandez has offered to coach the basketball team, however, the competition is intense.

    b. Ms. Hermandez has offered to coach the basketball team, however the competition is intense.

    c. Ms. Hermandez has offered to coach the team; however, the competition is intense.

    d. None of the Above.

Directions: for questions 5 - 10 choose the sentence with the correct punctuation and capitalization.

11. Choose the sentence with the correct punctuation and capitalization.

    a. The teacher just told us that it's time for the test.

    b. Although his' car was fairly new he sold it to the banker.

    c. She moved out of her parents' house into her's.

    d. Who's brand new Camaro is this parked on the lawn?

12. Choose the sentence with the correct punctuation and capitalization.

    a. I went to the supermarket: I bought chicken rice and fruits.

    b. Iv'e never been this much in love before: until you.

    c. I've just eaten these fruits; apples, peaches, plums and grapes.

    d. The worst vices are: prostitution, gambling and drug trafficking.

13. Choose the sentence with the correct punctuation and capitalization.

a. The writer J. K. Rowling is British.

b. Have you seen my best Friend Scott who lives next door?

c. J. R. R. Tolkien, wrote the Lord of the Rings.

d. The US president, Barak Obama, arrived yesterday.

14. Choose the sentence with the correct punctuation and capitalization.

a. This video game is not interesting said Bobby to his friend.

b. This Video game is not interesting, said Bobby, to his friend.

c. "This video game is not interesting." Said Bobby to his friend.

d. "This video game is not interesting," said Bobby to his friend.

15. Choose the sentence with the correct punctuation and capitalization.

a. James Smith, the president of the club, invited the members to a party.

b. The president of the club James Smith, invited the members to a party.

c. The president of the club James Smith invited the members to a party.

d. James Smith the president of the club invited the members to a party.

16. Combine the following two sentences into one sentence with the same meaning.

Lisa applies herself to her studies.
Lisa may achieve excellent grades.

a. Lisa may achieve excellent grades to apply herself to her studies.

b. If Lisa achieves good grades she may apply herself to her studies.

c. Lisa applies herself to her studies although she may achieve excellent grades.

d. Lisa may achieve excellent grades once she applies herself to her studies.

17. Combine the following two sentences into one sentence with the same meaning.

Richard took lessons in Spanish.
Richard wanted a job at the Spanish Embassy.

a. Richard took lessons in Spanish so that he wanted a job at the Spanish Embassy.

b. Richard took lessons in Spanish since he wanted a job at the Spanish Embassy.

c. Even if Richard wanted a job at the Spanish Embassy he took lessons in Spanish.

d. Having taken a job at the Spanish Embassy, Richard took lessons in Spanish.

18. Combine the following two sentences into one sentence with the same meaning.

The principal gives Bob a warning.
Bob does not disobey the rules.

    a. If the principal gives Bob a warning he does not disobey the rules.

    b. Bob does not disobey the rules but also the principal gives him a warning

    c. Even if the principal gives Bob a warning he does not disobey the rules.

    d. The principal gives Bob a warning so that he does not disobey the rules.

19. Combine the following two sentences into one sentence with the same meaning.

Linda was very late for school.
Linda missed an important subject.

    a. Because Linda missed an important subject she was very late for school.

    b. Linda missed an important subject so that she was late for school.

    c. Linda was so late for school that she missed an important subject.

    d. Although Linda was very late for school, she missed an important subject.

20. Combine the following two sentences into one sentence with the same meaning.

Mary worked hard.

Mary succeeded at her job.

  a. Mary succeeded at her job but she worked hard.

  b. Whenever Mary succeeded at her job she worked hard.

  c. Mary worked hard and thus she succeeded at her job.

  d. However hard Mary worked, she succeeded at her job.

Directions: For questions 21 - 24 below, you are given a topic sentence. Choose the sentence which best develops the given topic sentence.

21. Education is the pathway out of poverty.

  a. Getting a college education is very expensive.

  b. Over a billion people worldwide earn less than a dollar a day.

  c. Many children in poor countries do not have access to a good education.

  d. Having a college degree results in more earning potential.

22. Parents should ensure their children's safety near water bodies.

  a. Families should take trips to the beach together.

  b. CPR is one of the most basic first aid skills.

  c. Young children shouldn't be alone near water.

  d. The earth is divided into four major oceans.

23. Couples should be properly prepared before having children.

a. China restricts the number of children a couple may have.

b. There are thousands of children in state care.

c. No contraceptive method is 100 percent safe.

d. The financial and emotional burden must be considered.

24. The TOEFL test is an adequate assessment of English proficiency.

a. Nonnative speakers usually find English difficult to learn.

b. English is one of the most widely spoken world languages.

c. American universities require non-natives to pass the TOEFL.

d. The four skill areas are assessed using varied methodology.

25. A college degree is an essential requirement for a well-paying job.

a. US and UK colleges are among the best in the world.

b. Some persons complain that their salaries are inadequate.

c. A high-school diploma only gives access to entry-level jobs.

d. Many foreign universities offer scholarships to Americans.

Questions 26 - 30 refer to the following passage.

Man has been observing the natural environment for ages and has been using principles learned to advance and improve on various types of technology. <u>The development of gliders is one</u> (26) example. The evolution of gliders originated from man's fascination with bird flight. Gliders were developed after careful study of the flight pattern of birds. The first efforts to duplicate bird-like flying behavior happened from in the early 1800s. <u>In Britain, Sir George Cayley, studying birds, in flight</u> (27), attempted to understand the patterns observed and used the area of mathematics to formulate his observations. He was one first person to formulate mathematical theories about flying. He theorized that the wings, when set at particular angles, caused the bird <u>to ascend glide, or descend</u> (28). From his observations and theories he designed a type of glider and tested its ability to remain in flight, successfully so.

In later years experimenters would come up with their own theories based on their observations and calculations. <u>One sea captain, Jean Marie LeBris, kill an albatross</u> (29) to study its wings and then designed and successfully flew what was later called the LeBris glider in 1857. A German, Otto Lilienthal, went even further. He covered peeled willow wands with waxed cotton cloth in his glider design. This design made several thousand flights, with constant improvements. The art of making gliders <u>has been perfected</u> (30) over the years. Gliders nowadays are able to fly for hundreds of miles.

Read the passage below and look at the numbered, underlined phrases. Choose the answer that is written correctly for each underlined part.

26. Choose the correct version.

    a. The development of Gliders is one

    b. The development of gliders are one

    c. The development of gliders is some

    d. Correct as is.

Practice Test Questions 2

27. Choose the correct version.

   a. In Britain, Sir George Cayley, studying birds in flight

   b. In Britain; Sir George Cayley studying birds in flight

   c. In Britain Sir George Cayley, studying birds in flight

   d. Correct as is.

28. Choose the correct version.

   a. to ascend glide or descend

   b. to ascend, glide or descend

   c. to ascend, glide nor descend

   d. Correct as is.

29. Choose the correct version.

   a. One sea captain, Jean Marie LeBris, killed an albatross

   b. One sea captain – Jean Marie LeBris; kill an albatross

   c. One sea captain: Jean Marie LeBris: kills an albatross

   d. Correct as is.

30. Choose the correct version.

   a. have been perfected

   b. was been perfected

   c. has being perfected

   d. Correct as is.

Vocabulary

31. Because of its colorful fall _____, the maple is my favorite tree.

    a. Growth
    b. Branches
    c. Greenery
    d. Foliage

32. When Mr. Davis returned from southern Asia, he told us about the _____ that sometimes swept the area, bringing torrential rain.

    a. Monsoons
    b. Hurricanes
    c. Blizzards
    d. Floods

33. In heavily industrialized areas, the pollution of the air causes many to develop _____ diseases.

    a. Respiratory
    b. Cardiac
    c. Alimentary
    d. Circulatory

34. You can _____ some fires by covering them with dirt, while others require foam or water.

    a. Extinguish
    b. Distinguish
    c. Ignite
    d. Lessen

35. Through the use of powerful fans that circulate the heat over the food, _____ ovens work very efficiently.

   a. Microwave
   b. Broiler
   c. Convection
   d. Pressure

For questions 36 - 40, choose the word that best completes both sentences.

36. She always _____ people behind their back.
He _____ his opponents in his speeches.

   a. Offends
   b. Belittle
   c. Avoid
   d. Admire

37. They aren't exciting - all of the pictures are very _____.
His clothes are always very _____.

   a. Exciting
   b. Continuous
   c. Unforgiving
   d. Mundane

38. The auditorium was _____ when we arrived.
With 8 children, their house is always _____.

   a. Bedlam
   b. Placid
   c. Calm
   d. Noise

**39. I would like to _____ if possible.
They tried, but couldn't _____ the disaster.**

   a. Avert
   b. Promote
   c. Avenge
   d. Facilitate

**40. The water will soon _____.
It is all gone. The water _____ over the last hour.**

   a. Drip
   b. Dissipate
   c. Appear
   d. Degenerate

Answer Key

Reading

1. A
Choice B is incorrect; the author did not express their opinion on the subject matter. Choice C is incorrect, the author was not trying to prove a point, nor is the author trying to persuade.

2. C
Choice C is correct; historians believe it was brutal and bloody. Choice A is incorrect; there is no consensus that the Crusades achieved great things. Choice B is incorrect; it did not stabilize the Holy Lands. Choice D is incorrect, some historians do believe this was the purpose but not all historians.

3. D
The feudal system led to infighting. Choice A is incorrect, it had the opposite effect. Choice B is incorrect, though this is a good answer, it is not the best answer. The Church asked for volunteers not the Feudal Lords. Choice C is incorrect, it did have an effect on the Crusades.

4. A
Saracen was a generic term for Muslims widely used in Europe during the later medieval era.

5. B
This warranty does not cover a product that you have tried to fix yourself. From paragraph two, "This limited warranty does not cover ... any unauthorized disassembly, repair, or modification. "

6. C
ABC Electric could either replace or repair the fan, provided the other conditions are met. ABC Electric has the option to repair or replace.

7. B
The warranty does not cover a stove damaged in a flood.

From the passage, "This limited warranty does not cover any damage to the product from improper installation, accident, abuse, misuse, natural disaster, insufficient or excessive electrical supply, abnormal mechanical or environmental conditions."

A flood is an "abnormal environmental condition," and a natural disaster, so it is not covered.

8. A
A missing part is an example of defective workmanship. This is an error made in the manufacturing process. A defective part is not considered workmanship.

9. D
This question tests the reader's summarization skills. The other choices A, B, and C focus on portions of the second paragraph that are too narrow and do not relate to the specific portion of text in question. The complexity of the sentence may mislead students into selecting one of these answers, but rearranging or restating the sentence will lead the reader to the correct answer. In addition, choice A makes an assumption that may or may not be true about the intentions of the company, choice B focuses on one product rather than the idea of the products, and choice C makes an assumption about women that may or may not be true and is not supported by the text.

10. B
This question tests reader's attention to detail. If a reader selects A, he or she may have picked up on the use of the word "debate" and assumed, very logically, that the two are at odds because they are fighting; however, this is simply not supported in the text. Choice C also uses very specific quotes from the text, but it rearranges and gives them false meaning. The artists want to elevate their creations above the creations of other artists, thereby showing that they are "creative" and "innovative." Similarly, choice D takes phrases straight from the text and rearranges and confuses them. The artists are described as wanting to be "creative, innovative, individual people," not the women.

11. A
This question tests reader's vocabulary and summarization skills. This phrase, used by the author, may seem flippant and dismissive if readers focus on the word "whatever" and misinterpret it as a popular, colloquial term. In this way, Choices B and C may mislead the reader to selecting one of them by including the terms "unimportant" and "stupid," respectively. Choice D is a similar misreading, but doesn't make sense when the phrase is at the beginning of the passage and the entire passage is on media messages. Choice A is literarily and contextually appropriate, and the reader can understand that the author would like to keep the introduction focused on the topic the passage is going to discuss.

12. A
This question tests a reader's inference skills. The extreme use of the word "all" in choice B suggests that every single advertising company are working to be approachable, and while this is not only unlikely, the text specifically states that "more" companies have done this, signifying that they have not all participated, even if it's a possibility that they may some day. The use of the limiting word "only" in choice C lends that answer similar problems; women are still buying from companies who do not care about this message, or those companies would not be in business, and the passage specifies that "many" women are worried about media messages, but not all. Readers may find choice D logical, especially if they are looking to make an inference, and while this may be a possibility, the passage does not suggest or discuss this happening. Choice A is correct based on specifically because of the relation between "still working" in the answer and "will hopefully" and the extensive discussion on companies struggles, which come only with progress, in the text.

13. C
This question tests the reader's summarization skills. The entire passage is leading up to the idea that the president of the US may not have had grounds to assert his Fourteen Points when other countries had lost so much. Choice A is pretty directly inferred by the text, but it does not adequately summarize what the entire passage is trying to communicate. Choice B may also be inferred by the passage when it says that the war is "imminent," but it does not represent

the entire message, either. The passage does seem to be in praise of FDR, or at least in respect of him, but it does not in any way claim that he is the smartest president, nor does this represent the many other points included. Choice C is then the obvious answer, and most directly relates to the closing sentences which it rewords.

14. C
This question tests the reader's attention to detail. The passage does state that choices A and B are true, and while those statements are in proximity to the explanation for why the war started, they are not the reason given. Choice D is a mix up of words used in the passage, which says that the largest powers were in play but not that this fact somehow started the war. The passage does make a direct statement that a domino effect started the war, supporting choice C as the correct answer.

15. A
This question tests the reader's understanding of functions in writing. Throughout the passage, it states that leaders of other nations were hesitant to accept generous or peaceful terms because of the grievances of the war, and the great loss of life was chief among these. While the passage does touch on the devastation of deadly weapons (B), the use of this raw, emotional fact serves a larger purpose, and the focus of the passage is not weapons. While readers may indeed consider who lost the most soldiers (C) when, so many countries were involved and the inequalities of loss are mentioned in the passage, there is no discussion of this in the passage. Choice D is related to A, but choice A is more direct and relates more to the passage.

16. B
This question tests the reader's vocabulary skills. Choice A may seem appealing to readers because it is phonetically similar to "catalyzed," but the two are not related in any other way. Choice C makes sense in context, but if plugged in to the sentence creates a redundancy that doesn't make sense. Choice D does also not make sense contextually, even if the reader may consider that funds were needed to create more weaponry, especially if it was advanced.

17. A
Victoria is about 5 miles from Burnaby.

18. B
The Village Hall is about 5 miles from Victoria.

19. A
The correct order of ingredients is brown sugar, baking soda and chocolate chips.

20. B
Sturdy: strong, solid in structure or person. In context, Stir in chocolate chips by hand with a *sturdy* wooden spoon.

21. A
Disperse: to scatter in different directions or break up. In context, Stir until the chocolate chips and nuts are evenly *dispersed*.

22. B
You can stop stirring the nuts when they are evenly distributed. From the passage, "Stir until the chocolate chips and nuts are evenly dispersed."

23. B
Choice A is incorrect as the Monster killed Frankenstein, not the other way around. Choice B is correct, Frankenstein is dead. Choice C is incorrect - Mary Shelley is the author. Choice D is incorrect, the person is called Frankenstein.

24. C
The speaker 'suspended' from following through on his duty to destroy the monster due to curiosity and compassion. The other choices may seem reasonable, but are not explicitly given in the passage.

25. D
All the choices are correct. Frankenstein's monster destroys Frankenstein by

    a. By killing Frankenstein

    b. By letting himself be the monster everyone sees him as

    c. By destroying everything Frankenstein loved

Computational Mathematics

1. C
8974 − 8256 = 718

2. A
4404 / 8 = 550.5

3. D
274 * 139 = 38086

4. B
3567 + 99 = 3666

5. A
2 + a number divided by 7.
(2 + X) divided by 7.
(2 + X)/7

6. A
60/x = 75/100
60 * 100/X = 75
6000/75 = X
X = 80

7. C
71 ÷ 1000 = 0.071.

8. A
.33 × .59 = .195

9. A
Collect like terms, 7x = 47 + 9 = 56,
divide both sides by 7
x = 8

10. C
The ten thousandths place in 1.7389 will be the 4th decimal place, 9.

11. A
.87 − .48 = 0.39.

Practice Test Questions 2   277

12. C
Forty nine thousandths will place the '9' in the 3rd decimal place, 0.049.

13. C
a. 3/4 * 2/2 = 6/8
b. 3/4 * 3/3 = 9/12
c. 3/4 * 4/4 = 12/16 - Incorrect
d. 3/4 * 7/7 = 21/28

14. D
a. 84/231 = 12/33 > 1/3
b. 6/35 = 1/5 < 1/3
c. 3/22 = 1/7 < 1/3
d. b and c are less than 1/3

15. C
Here are the choices:
a. 1
b. √2 = 1.414
c. 3/2 = 1.5   Largest number
d. 4/3 = 1.33

16. B
Collecting similar terms (algebraic addition).
2b + 9b – 5b = 11b - 5b = 6b

17. C
4.7 + .9 + .01 = 5.61.

18. D
60/100 = 12/X
60 = 12 * 100/X
60X = 1200
X = 1200/60
X = 20.

19. D
.84/.7 = 1.2

20. C
4120 – 3216 = 904

21. D
2417 + 1004 = 3421

22. B
0.12 + 2/5 - 3/5, Convert decimal to fraction to get 3/25 + 2/5 - 3/5, = (3 + 10)/25 - 15/25, = - 2/25.

23. D
700,653 – 70,099 = 630,554

24. A
0.25 + 2 1/3 + 2/3, first convert decimal to fraction, 1/4 + 1/3 + 2/3, (3 + 4 + 8)/12, = 15/12 = 5/4 = 1 1/4

25. B
10% of 300 = 30 and 50% of 20 = 10 so 30 + 10 = 40.

Applied Mathematics

1. C
1 hour is equal to 3,600 seconds and 1 kilometer is equal to 1000 meters.

Since this train travels 72 kilometers per hour, this means that it covers 72,000 meters in 3,600 seconds.

If it travels 72,000 meters in 3,600 seconds

It travels x meters in 12 seconds

By cross multiplication: x = 72,000 • 12 / 3,600

x = 240 meters

2. B
Total Volume = Volume of large cylinder - Volume of small cylinder

Volume of a cylinder = area of base • height = $\pi r^2 \cdot h$

Total Volume = (π * 12² * 10) - (π * 6² * 5) = 1440π - 180π

= 1260π in³

3. A
Let us first mention the money Tony spent: $80

Now we need to find the money Tony earned:

He had 15 dozen eggs = 15 * 12 = 180 eggs. 16 eggs were broken. So,

Remaining number of eggs that Tony sold = 180 – 16 = 164.

Total amount he earned for selling 164 eggs = 164 * 0.54 = $88.56.

As a summary, he spent $80 and earned $88.56.

The profit is the difference: 88.56 - 80 = $8.56

Percentage profit is found by proportioning the profit to the money he spent:

8.56•100/80 = 10.7%

Checking the answers, we round 10.7 to the nearest whole number: 11%

4. B
Number of absent students = 83 – 72 = 11

Percentage of absent students is found by proportioning the number of absent students to total number of students in the class = (11 * 100)/83 = 13.25

Checking the answers, we round 13.25 to the nearest whole number: 13%

5. A
P = 200, r = 15%, I = 245 – 200 = $45, t =? First convert the rate to a decimal, 15% = 0.15. I = P x r x t. Therefore, 45 = 200 x 0.15 x t, 45 = 30t, t = 45/30 = 1.5. She will have to wait for 1½ years for his $200 to earn $45 interest to become $245.

6. C
I = 600, r = 3, t = 2 and P = ? Using the formula, P = 100 x interest/ r x t

100 x 600/ 3 x 2 = 60000/6 = 10,000. The original amount deposited was $10,000

7. B
Based on this graph, a person that is 85 or older will make 31.3 visits to the hospital every year.

8. A
Based on this graph, the number of visits per year is going up as age goes up, so we can expect a person that is 95 to have more than 31.3 visits to the hospital each year.

9. A
The formula of the volume of cylinder is the base area multiplied by the height. As the formula:

Volume of a cylinder = $\pi r^2 h$. Where π is 3.142, r is radius of the cross sectional area, and h is the height.

We know that the diameter is 5 meters, so the radius is 5/2 = 2.5 meters.

The volume is: V = 3.142 * 2.5² * 12 = 235.65 m³.

10. C
The large cube is made up of 8 smaller cubes with 5 cm sides. The volume of a cube is found by the third power of the length of one side.
Volume of the large cube = Volume of the small cube•8

= (5³)•8 = 125•8

= 1000 cm³

There is another solution for this question. Find the side length of the large cube. There are two cubes rows with 5 cm length for each. So, one side of the large cube is 10 cm.

The volume of this large cube is equal to 10³ = 1000 cm³

11. A
The line is pointing towards numbers greater than 2. The equation is therefore, X > 2.

12. C
Pythagorean Theorem:
(Hypotenuse)² = (Perpendicular)² + (Base)²
$h^2 = a^2 + b^2$

Given: a = 6, h = 10
$h^2 = a^2 + b^2$
$b^2 = h^2 - a^2$

$b^2 = 10^2 + 6^2$
$b^2 = 100 - 36$
$b^2 = 64$
$b = 8$

13. D

As shown in the figure, two parallel lines intersecting with a third line with angle of 75°.

$x = 75°$ (corresponding angles)

$x + y = 180°$ (supplementary angles) ... inserting the value of x here:

$y = 180° - 75°$
$y = 105°$

14. D

Two parallel lines (m & side AB) intersected by side AC. This means that 50° and a angles are interior angles. So:
$a = 50°$ (interior angles).

15. D

We have a circle given with diameter 8 cm and a square located within the circle. We are asked to find the area of the circle for which we only need to know the length of the radius that is the half of the diameter.
Area of circle = πr^2 ... r = 8/2 = 4 cm

Area of circle = $\pi \cdot 4^2$

= 16π cm² ... As we notice, the inner square has no role in this question.

16. B

Perimeter of a parallelogram is the sum of the sides.
Perimeter = $2(l + b)$
Perimeter = $2(3 + 10)$, 2×13
Perimeter = 26 cm.

17. C

87% = 87/100 = 0.87

18. C
Volume of a cylinder is π x r² x h
Diameter = 5 ft. so radius is 2.5 ft.
Volume of cylinder= π x 2.5² x 2
= π x 6.25 x 2 = 12.5 π
Approximate π to 3.142
Volume of the cylinder = 39.25

Volume of a rectangle = height X width X length.
= 5 X 5 X 4 = 100

Total volume = Volume of rectangular solid + volume of cylinder
Total volume = 100 + 39.25
Total volume = 139.25 ft³ or about 140 ft³

19. D
The jacket costs $545.00 so we can round up to $550. 10% of $550 is 55. We can round down to $50, which is easier to work with. $550 - $50 is $500. The jacket will cost about $500.

The actual cost will be 10% X 545 = $54.50
545 – 54.50 = $490.50

20. C
We see that two legs of a right triangle form by Peter's movements and we are asked to find the length of the hypotenuse. We use the Pythagorean Theorem:

(Hypotenuse)² = (Perpendicular)² + (Base)²
h² = a² + b²

Given: 3² + 4² = h²
h² = √25
h = 5

21. D
P= $5,500, t = 3 years, r = 5%, I = ? convert rate to decimal and 5% = 0.05
I = 5,500 x 0.05 x 3 = 825. Total amount in the account = principal + interest or 5,500 + 825 = $6,325

Practice Test Questions 2

22. D
First calculate total square feet, which is 15 * 24 = 360 ft². Next, convert this value to square yards, (1 yards² = 9 ft²) which is 360/9 = 40 yards². At $0.50 per square yard, the total cost is 40 * 0.50 = $20.

23. B
Flat Screen TVs are the third best-selling product.

24. B
The two products that are closest in the number of sales, are Flat Screen TVs and Radar Detectors.

25. B
I = ?, r = 3%, t = 2 years, P = 6000. Convert rate to decimal. 3% = 0.03. Then plug in variables into the simple interest formula. I = P x r x t, I = 6000 x 0.03 x 2, I = $360.

Language

1. B
A colon is used before a list of items following an independent clause.

2. A
A comma is used to introduce short quotations or proverbs.

3. A
The colon is used in the salutation of a formal business letter.

4. B
An apostrophe is placed before the letter "s" to indicate singular possession.

5. A
A parenthesis is used to set off asides and explanations only when the material is not essential or when it consists of one or more sentences.

6. C
The dash is used when the speaker cannot continue.

7. B
The dash is used to show a closed range of values.

8. C
A hyphen is used with fractions used as adjectives.

9. B
Ellipsis (…) is used to indicate passage of time.

10. A
"However" generally has a comma before and after.

11. A
Choice A uses the apostrophe correctly in "it's." All the other choices have incorrect apostrophe use.

12. A
Choice A uses the colon correctly. Choice B uses the incorrect form, "Iv'e." Choice C uses a semicolon instead of a colon. Choice D uses the colon incorrectly.

13. A
Choice A has correct punctuation and capitalization. Choice B incorrectly capitalizes "friend." Choice C uses a comma incorrectly. In choice D, "president" should be capitalized .

14. D
Choice A is incorrect because it does not use quotation marks. Choice B does not use quotation marks and incorrectly places a comma after Bobby. Choice C incorrectly places a period after Bobby.

15. A
Choice A is the only choice which uses the comma correctly.

16. D
17. B
18. D
19. C
20. C
21. D
22. C
23. D

24. D

25. C

26. D
The phrase is correct as is. Choice A incorrectly capitalizes "gliders." Choice B incorrectly uses "are." Choice C incorrectly uses "some."

27. A
Choice A uses commas correctly. Choice B incorrectly uses a semi colon instead of a comma. Choice C omits a comma after "Britain."

28. B
Choice B is the only choice that uses commas correctly.

29. A
Choice A uses commas correctly. Choice B uses the dash where it is not needed, and a semi colon instead of a comma. Choice C uses colons instead of comma.

30. D
The phrase is correct as is, and uses the past perfect correctly. The other choices all use the past perfect incorrectly.

Vocabulary

31. D
Foliage: plant leaves

32. A
Monsoons: a seasonal prevailing wind in the region of South and Southeast Asia, blowing from the southwest between May and September and bringing rain

33. A
Respiratory: of, relating to, or affecting respiration or the organs of respiration.

34. A
Extinguish: cause (a fire or light) to cease to burn or shine.

35. C
Convection: the movement caused within a fluid by the tendency of hotter and therefore less dense material to rise, and colder, denser material to sink under the influence of gravity, which consequently results in transfer of heat.

36. B
Belittle: make (someone or something) seem unimportant.

37. D
Mundane: Ordinary; not new.

38. A
Bedlam: A place or situation of chaotic uproar, and where confusion prevails.

39. A
Avert: To ward off, or prevent, the occurrence or effects of.

40. B
Dissipate: disperse or scatter.

Conclusion

CONGRATULATIONS! You have made it this far because you have applied yourself diligently to practicing for the exam and no doubt improved your potential score considerably! Getting into a good school is a huge step in a journey that might be challenging at times but will be many times more rewarding and fulfilling. That is why being prepared is so important.

Study then Practice and then Succeed!

Good Luck!

Register for Free Updates and More Practice Test Questions

Register your purchase at
https://www.test-preparation.ca/register/
for updates, free test tips and more practice test questions.

Visit us Online!

www.test-preparation.ca

https://www.facebook.com/CompleteTestPreparation/

https://www.youtube.com/user/MrTestPreparation

Online Resources

How to Prepare for a Test - The Ultimate Guide

https://www.test-preparation.ca/the-ultimate-guide-to-test-preparation-strategy/

Learning Styles - The Complete Guide

https://www.test-preparation.ca/learning-styles/

Test Anxiety Secrets!

https://www.test-preparation.ca/how-to-overcome-test-anxiety/

Time Management on a Test

https://www.test-preparation.ca/test-tactics-the-time-wise-approach/

Flash Cards - The Complete Guide

https://www.test-preparation.ca/test-preparation-with-flash-cards/

Test Preparation Video Series

https://www.test-preparation.ca/video-series-on-test-preparation-multiple-choice-strategies-and-how-to-study/

How to Memorize - The Complete Guide

https://www.test-preparation.ca/a-guide-to-memorizing-anything-easily-and-painlessly/

www.ingramcontent.com/pod-product-compliance
Lightning Source LLC
Chambersburg PA
CBHW071807080526
44589CB00012B/725